AF248878

Forgotten Dreams

FORGOTTEN DREAMS

Ritual in
American Popular Art

Thomas St. John

VANTAGE PRESS
New York / Washington / Atlanta
Los Angeles / Chicago

For my mother and father, ever faithful

FIRST EDITION

Copyright © 1987 by Thomas St. John

Published by Vantage Press, Inc.
516 West 34th Street, New York, New York 10001

Manufactured in the United States of America
ISBN: 0-533-06686-7

Library of Congress Catalog Card No.: 85-90186

Contents

Nothing almost sees miracles

But misery. I know 'tis from Cordelia,
Who hath most fortunately been informed
Of my obscured course—and "shall find time
From this enormous state, seeking to give
Losses their remedies"—All weary and o'erwatched,
Take vantage, heavy eyes, not to behold
This shameful lodging.
Fortune, good night; smile once more, turn thy wheel.

—King Lear

Preface: Scythes and Cannon Fire

As a freelance writer, I have deliberately chosen subjects that are all but forbidden to professional academics. Even the *manner* in which I speak of these subjects is strictly, if discreetly, taboo in the Ivory Tower. This school censorship may be admirable and politic—in the way that collaboration always is—but it encourages ominous and sinister silences. The American people are correct in being wary of their "official" intellectuals. Perhaps only an independent writer is free to know Nathaniel Hawthorne's and Herman Melville's concern for the traps laid for them by the academic and literary set that oppressed them. Hawthorne's and Melville's most spirited and creative—if sadly limited—response to this was to invent an entirely traditional, yet deplorable and inconceivably comic hoax, or trap of their own, for the pompous and the vain. Academics who have criticized these great writers ever since have—to a man—walked into the trap blindly. Since the literary set did not dare to "discover" Melville until thirty years after his death in virtually total obscurity, there is a kind of poetic justice in his stratagem.

When Napoleon's armies overran Germany, Jakob and Wilhelm Grimm searched the Hessian countryside for their beloved household tales, finding solace and faith in the past, if not in the desolate present. In "The Father's Legacies," a population is described, living on an isolated island. They have never heard of a scythe. When they wanted to reap their corn, they brought out cannon and shot it down. Finally a man comes to the island with a scythe, and the populace is struck dumb by its gentle craft. The islanders purchase this common scythe—at great cost. The mystery of lost time, perhaps, also needs the cradling of stout scythes—not more glorious cannon fire—to reap those insights otherwise buried alive. I hope the following six formal chapters are in keeping with the spirit of Nathaniel Hawthorne when he said, "I would come, as if to gather up the white ashes of those who had perished at the stake, and to tell the world—the wrong being now atoned for—how much had perished there which it had never yet known how to praise."

Brattleboro, Vermont
May 6, 1985

Acknowledgments

"Lyman Frank Baum's Land of Oz: Allegory of Political Terror" first appeared as "Lyman Frank Baum: Looking Back to the Promised Land" in the University of Utah's *Western Humanities Review*, XXXVI, No. 4 (Winter 1982). The chapter "Walter Elias Disney: The Cartoon as Race Fantasy" was printed in the *Ball State University Forum XXIV*, No. 3 (Summer 1983). The author is very grateful for the encouragement and the skills of the *Review's* editors Jack Garlington and Robert Shapard and the *Forum's* Frances M. Rippy. The suggestions and ideas of Vantage Press's editor Barbara Wild served to clarify the text.

Thanks are also extended to Macmillan Publishing Company, for permission to reprint an extract from "Among School Children" and an extract from "The Circus Animals' Desertion" both of which are by W. B. Yeats; the Houghton Library, for permission to quote from a letter written by Nathaniel Hawthorne; the *New England Quarterly*, for permission to reprint an extract from Edwin H. Cady's "The Artistry of Jonathan Edwards"; *American Literature*, for permission to quote from Richard Van Der Beets "The Indian Captivity Narrative as Ritual"; Farrar, Straus and Giroux, Inc., for permission to quote from "For the Union Dead," by Robert Lowell; Grove Press, for permission to use an excerpt from *Black Skin, White Masks*, by Frantz Fanon; Thomas B. Adams, for permission to quote from his column, "History Looks Ahead"; Henry M. Littlefield and the University of Pennsylvania, for permission to reprint an extract from Mr. Littlefield's "The

Wizard of Oz: Parable on Populism"; Harcourt Brace Jovanovich, Inc., and Faber and Faber Publishers for permission to reprint an extract from T. S. Eliot's "Little Gidding"; Warner Bros. Music, for permission to reprint portions of the lyrics of "As Time Goes By," by Herman Hupfeld, and "It Had To Be You," by Gus Kahn and Isham Jones; Shapiro Bernstein and Co., Inc., for permission to reprint two lines from the lyrics of "S-H-I-N-E," by Cecil Mack and Lew Brown; and Warner Brothers, Inc., for permission to use dialogue from *Casablanca*.

Forgotten Dreams

1

Lyman Frank Baum's Land of Oz: Allegory of Political Terror

          —John Greenleaf Whittier

After Frank Baum died in 1919, his widow took the original manuscript of *The Wonderful Wizard of Oz* from an attic trunk in Hollywood, California, and burned it, and other papers, in a backyard incinerator. She later explained that "she could see no point to cluttering up the attic with a lot of worthless paper."[1] But Baum's allegory already compelled the conscience of many Americans. That few dared to question the political sources of the allegory served Baum's purposes as well, for he needed to keep a safe distance from the idol-worshipping and the innocent. Baum seemed to be an ordinary man, leading an ordinary life. But the image of the bluff, hearty salesman masked an astute observer of the Gilded Age, which surrounded and so degraded him. He wisely chose never to reveal this deeper self. Baum was idealistic, generous to a fault, a pacifist, and a persistent dreamer. His greatest torment was the impressive level of racial violence in the United States, especially as regarded blacks, Indians, the Irish, and the Chinese.

Sadly inarticulate in many ways, Frank Baum was trapped

in a society that believed in white supremacy, defined racial terror as patriotism, and enforced the segregation of both men and ideas. A man of no brilliant academic achievement, Baum yet remained sensitive to the corrosive effects of slavery on the white conscience and to the intellectual degeneracy attendant upon belief in white supremacy. Baum confronted problems of moral definition that more clear-thinking and better-informed men had found utterly insurmountable. What could he affirm in that labyrinth of the Gilded Age?

Frank Baum temporarily escaped an intolerable American reality by creating a political allegory—*The Wonderful Wizard of Oz*—in the summer of 1899. In this effort to solve on paper, if not in fact, a number of acutely American conflicts, Baum amassed a cultural treasure house, a historical watershed containing some of the painful, dislocated trends and conflicts that preoccupied his fellow citizens. The fantasy creatures assembled in Oz bear some resemblance to the figures in the contemporary political cartoons, which Baum knew so well from his days as a newspaper editor. Satirical in the spirit of Jonathan Swift—and as deceptively innocent—*The Wonderful Wizard of Oz* is by turns matter-of-fact, sardonic, bitter, manic, whimsical, and tender, with occasional punning and, most unhappily, direct appeals to public attitudes of white supremacy.

Concealing his doubts and troubles, unresolved, in an ostensibly innocent story for children, Baum exploited a deep need of the white middle classes to put a happy face on terror. By diverting the concerns of his uneasy conscience into an indubiously well-intended allegory, Baum won an immense popular success. But Baum's satire completely missed its mark: the public refused to acknowledge his references to race issues and turned the political allegory into a piece of pure sentimentalism. The cost of personal safety in obscurity for Frank Baum was ultimately paid for in failed satire. No one knew the shame of compromise more than the author himself.

This shame certainly never paralyzed Frank Baum—who

was neither professor, nor artiste, but salesman, selling himself cheerfully and habitually. Indeed, Baum is explicitly at pains to deny shame and responsibility alike in his introduction to *The Wonderful Wizard of Oz*.[2] While easing his conscience by projecting his racial terrors and guilts into stories for children, Frank Baum denies that there is any manipulation or violence in his "series of newer 'wonder tales' in which the stereotyped genie, dwarf and fairy are eliminated, together with all the horrible and blood-curdling incidents devised by their authors to point a fearsome moral to each tale." This is an ingenious disclaimer indeed. He says, "the heartaches and nightmares are left out." In denying his responsibility, Baum resorts to this astounding piece of sophistry and glib assertion: "Modern education includes morality; therefore the modern child seeks only entertainment in its wonder-tales and gladly dispenses with all disagreeable incidents." But all the wishing in the world cannot make it so, and Frank Baum could not forget the blood-curdling affairs of the Gilded Age.[3]

The Oz fantasy is the chronicle of a child's journey from civilization to a fabulous land. As a child himself—born on May 15, 1856—Baum had often journeyed with his father from their home near Syracuse, New York, riding in the buckboard to the Allegheny reservation of the Seneca Indians to the west. The impressive Allegheny geography is clearly reflected in the later allegory:

> . . . The grant was, in effect, a sheltered sliver of fertile bottom-land, bounded on the east by the river itself, a hundred and fifty yards wide and up to six feet deep, and on the west by steep, ravine-cut, green cliffs that climbed five hundred feet to a razor-backed ridge. The cliffs swept in to within a few feet of the river above and below the grant, effectively sealing it off from unwanted horsemen and foot travellers.
>
> The principal way of access to the grant was an awkward Indian trail that cut north across the razor-back

hills, up and down the ravines, from the mouth of Conewango Creek. From Cornplanter's Town the trail proceeded up the west bank of the Allegheny River to the Indian towns in the reservation at Genesinguhta and Ichsua. Pinched in between cliffs and water, or scaling steep ravine slopes, this path was often blocked by snow and mud and rock slides in the winter and in the spring and the summer by swamps, fallen trees, and underbrush.[4]

In the early days of the oil industry, Baum's father had made a fortune in Pennsylvania, beginning as a coopersmith making barrels and ultimately becoming one of the independents whose careers were ended by David Rockefeller. Benjamin Baum's company town was Bradford, Pennsylvania. A few miles from Bradford, across the state line in New York, lay the Allegheny reservation. After their journey, Benjamin would negotiate oil land leases and his son was free to roam. Tutored privately at home because of a congenitally weak heart, Frank Baum spent hours wandering through the fields and forests. He was a markedly daydreaming youth and readily absorbed the romantic tales of Ireland that his mother told him. These fables prepared him to write and adapt the Irish melodramas that he staged and acted in during his twenties.[5] His father also told him stories about the old days in the oil fields and how the Seneca used to live on the land.

Following an adolescent exploration of newspaper work, and with the help of his father, Frank Baum took a job in Bradford with the weekly newspaper, the *Era*. He still spent his leisure time roaming the forests, making up stories as he went. Just north of Bradford lay the Seneca reservation. A few miles to the south lay the village of Cyclone, Pennsylvania. It is not surprising that the later Land of Oz is reached by way of a cyclone. Both the child and the man enjoyed comic literalism.[6]

In relating Dorothy's first journey to the Emerald City, Baum describes the struggle with the Kalidahs—creatures half bear and mostly tiger. Eventually the Kalidahs fall into a deep ravine, along with the tree that had served as a bridge over the chasm. Baum most likely derived this scene directly from Charles Brockden Brown's *Edgar Huntly; or, Memoirs of a Sleep-Walker* (1799). Brown's tree-trunk bridge, narrow escape, and panther scene evidently so captured the popular imagination of the nineteenth century that even in Baum's time, one hundred years later, a patent-medicine company in New York used it to advertise their products in a widely distributed broadside.

It is also possible that Baum derived his "cliff-hanger" episode from a source other than Brockden Brown, namely, Washington Irving's "Rip Van Winkle": "In old times, say the Indian traditions, there was a kind of Manitou or Spirit, who kept about the wildest recesses of the Catskill Mountains, and took a mischievous pleasure in wreaking all kinds of evils and vexations upon the red men. Sometimes he would assume the form of a bear, a panther, or a deer, lead the bewildered hunter a weary chase through tangled forests and among ragged rocks; and then spring off with a loud ho! ho! leaving him aghast on the brink of a beetling precipice or raging torrent."[7]

Between Baum's early years in the oil fields and his Chicago middle years, the most significant events concerning *The Wonderful Wizard of Oz* came during his residence in Dakota Territory. He moved with his family to the frontier village of Aberdeen, in present-day South Dakota, in July 1888. The proprietor of a novelty store, Baum's Bazaar, he was polite, patient and well dressed. Sitting on the dusty wooden sidewalk, he told stories to children—some of which he would publish in later years. Baum joined the Episcopal church and acted in a play called *Everybody's Friend*. When his five-and-dime failed because of the economic depression, he served as the editor of the *Saturday Pioneer*, increasing his awareness of local, territorial, and national politics. In editorials and a comedy column called "Our Landlady," Baum spoke of Indian affairs. One recent scholar has claimed that "Baum's editorials on the Indian situation were the least tolerant of all his work."[8]

Only the deepening depression caused Baum to abandon Aberdeen.

Gen. George A. Custer, described in 1873 as "a cold-blooded, untruthful and unprincipled man . . . universally despised by all the officers of his regiment," was a hero in Aberdeen.[9] In the summer of 1874, Custer had led the expedition that "discovered" gold in the Black Hills of the Dakotas. It was the subsequent attack on this land by white fortune-seekers that triggered the last of the Indian wars. This conflict enabled boom towns like Aberdeen to flourish. During his years in Dakota, Baum witnessed the Oklahoma land rush, as well as the dismantling of the Great Sioux Reservation, the Ghost Dance, the murder of Sitting Bull, and the slaughter at nearby Wounded Knee in December 1890.

Eight decades of increasingly effective sentimentalization obscure the fact, but the first readers of Baum's book realized that the Land of Oz reflected the Black Hills. Frank Baum's allegory corresponds roughly to the present-day states of Kansas, Nebraska, North and South Dakota, and Montana, and part of Canada. The original popularity of *The Wonderful Wizard of Oz* was fired by the desperate need of the white middle classes to find entertainment, respectability, and even more profits in that sordid land grab for gold "from the grass-roots down," as the late-lamented Custer had phrased it. The immense popularity of the book attracted the usual imitators, who tried to cash in on its success. The most important of them, Eva Katharine Gibson's *Zauberlinda; or, The Wise Witch*, actually names the Black Hills.[10]

The Yellow Brick Road has entered the American language as a symbol for the path to success, but the satiric Frank Baum originally intended the symbol as something less cheerful. He was well acquainted with the folly of the Black Hills gold-rushers looking for instant paradise. Baum may have been a persistent dreamer, but he knew the price of greed when he saw it. The symbol itself is derived from many distinct sources. Undoubtedly there is the memory of some physical yellow brick road in it. There is the Yellowstone Country or

Yellowstone River. "Yellow stone" meant a gold nugget.

"The Yellow Brick Road" refers to the famed Bozeman Road, which gave prospectors the easiest access to the gold fields of Montana, Virginia City, and the Last Chance Gulch. The original Bozeman Trail had been abandoned due to the successful resistance known as Red Cloud's War, which had forced the razing of Forts Phil Kearny, Reno, and C. F. Smith and the signing of the Fort Laramie Treaty.[11] This is the treaty that Custer violated by cutting a path through the Black Hills for his wagons on his gold-finding mission. Custer's path came to be known as The Thieves' Road. The deep resentment of this attack on the sacred ground also became part of the Yellow Brick Road.

The Winged Monkeys are Frank Baum's satire of the old Northwest Mounted Police, the precursors of the Royal Canadian Mounted Police. At the turn of the century, an aura of romance, adventure, and high honor was attached to the force: "A Mountie always gets his man." But for the Irish Baum, they could only be just more British police. Indeed, the Northwest Mounted Police were modeled in part on the Irish Constabulary and formed in direct response to American Fenian raids into British territory in Canada.[12]

The proud hallmark of the uniform of the Northwest Mounted Police was the scarlet tunic, which provided the brilliant and unmistakable warning to evil-doers. The original color plates of *The Wonderful Wizard of Oz* show the leader of the Winged Monkeys wearing the distinctive flat, round "pillbox" forage cap with the red band, the narrow visor, and the chin strap. Baum gives the Winged Monkeys the gift of flight, in recognition of the fact that the Mounties did not operate from fixed points, or forts, but roamed widely, in order to reassure the far-flung settlers that they could actually be protected. This symbol may well be another instance of Baum's humorous literalism; he may have heard some random malcontent refer to the Mounted Police as "winged monkeys."[13]

As to the *moral* hallmark of the Northwest Mounted Police: "An interesting fact was that this was to be a civil force in uniform, not a military organization subject to the Queen's regulations, but dependent for discipline upon the personality of the officers, the esprit de corps that would be generated and the *noblesse oblige* idea that would emerge in the course of service."[14] These Mounted Police were to be above partisan politics, religion, and race. It nearly worked.

The trouble was that the police did in fact represent the interests of a constituted authority in acquiring land for "the granary of the Empire." Frank Baum debunks the notion that the Mounted Police were somehow finer or purer than other law-enforcement agencies or politically independent by placing the Winged Monkeys—former slaves themselves—at the mercy of anyone in possession of the Golden Cap. Frank Baum may have told stories to children, but he knew that honor is sold for gold. If you possess the Golden Cap, you get three wishes.

In Aberdeen, the Mounted Police were unpopular because they were thought to be sheltering Sitting Bull, who had fled to Canada early in 1877, soon after the Battle of the Little Big Horn and the death of Custer. American settlers commonly perceived the situation in this manner. The American editor of the *Fort Benton Record* expressed the typical attitude in commenting on a chief of the Blackfeet: "Crow-Foot has always been the leader of noted murderers, and is responsible for the death of more than one emigrant and prospector, yet this red butcher has been the pet of the Mounted Police ever since the latter arrived in the country."[15]

It is possible Baum combined his satire of the Mounted Police with another group seen in opposition to his neighbors:

Baum makes these Winged Monkeys into an Oz substitute for the Plains Indians. Their leader says, "Once . . . we were a free people, living happily in the great forest, flying from tree to tree, eating nuts and fruit, and doing just as we pleased without calling anybody master. This," he explains, "was many years ago,

long before Oz came out of the clouds to rule over this
land." But like many Indian tribes Baum's monkeys are
not inherently bad; their actions depend wholly upon
the bidding of others. . . . Says the Monkey King, "We
belong to this country alone, and cannot leave it." The
same could be said with equal truth of the first Americans.[16]

The Shifting Sands, The Great Sandy Waste, The Deadly
Desert, and The Impassable Desert are Frank Baum's collective representation of that vast area including the Great
Plains and the Southwest, which emigrants then called the
great American desert. The sudden absence of forests beyond
the Missouri River made the area seem blasted, barren, unfit
for civilized living. Early Spanish explorers called it "the
northern mystery."[17] The soaring and plummeting tempera-
tures, the cyclones, blizzards, the crop-killing drought, dead-
level horizon, the sky, and the silence were fearsome. Robert
Louis Stevenson called it an "infinity." It drove more than
one pioneer insane.

The great American desert inspired a religious awe;
James Fenimore Cooper expressed this sentiment: "The glorious works of God are daily cut down and destroyed, and the
hand of man seems to be upraised in contempt of his mighty
will. They tell me there are fearful signs of what we may all
come to to be met with west and south of the Great
Lakes. . . . I mean the spots marked by the vengeance of
heaven, or which, perhaps, have been raised up as solemn
warnings to the thoughtless and wasteful, hereaways. They
call them prairies. . . ."[18]

In *The Wonderful Wizard of Oz*, the Shifting Sands, the
Great Sandy Waste, and so forth served to remind the original
readers of such actual regions as the Sand Hills of central
Nebraska. One resident affectionately termed this area "the
very worst country on the face of God's green earth," but the
newspapers encouraged its settlement with "Come to the
Arcadia and El Dorado, the Elysium and Hesperides of the

world!"[19] Frank Baum may also have been thinking of the Great Sand Hills of Canada, just across the border, in creating this symbol. This region was sacred to the Blackfeet as the place where spirits went after death, to live a shadow existence with no happiness and no sadness. It was there that Sitting Bull met peaceably with Crowfoot, naming his eight-year-old son after this chief. The possibility of an alliance caused many American settlers some anxiety.

Frank Baum's four deserts "that surround this land of Oz" are not entirely useless, for "by this means Oz is protected from foreign peoples—many of them far from amiable." The road leading into this is "a long journey, through a country that is sometimes pleasant and sometimes dark and terrible." And again: "The road is straight to the South, but it is said to be full of dangers to travelers. There are wild beasts in the woods, and a race of queer men who do not like strangers to cross their country." In the sixth book of the Oz series, Baum describes the land as completely cut off from civilization by "a Barrier of Invisibility that would protect the kingdom from further invasion."

In creating "great protective desert barriers" for his political allegory, Baum recognizes a long tradition in the white settlement of this continent: creating a "buffer state" from an unattractive land by filling it with the poor, the immigrant, the useless, the despised. Governor Donegan of New York in 1687 tried to persuade some Christian Indians living on the Saint Lawrence River to return to Saratoga and form a barrier between Albany and the hostile French.[20] In the eighteenth century, the English colonists kept the Irish and the Germans on their frontiers. Thomas Paine, fearful that the Spanish might conquer the South by offering American slaves better conditions if they rebelled, suggested that the freed Negroes might "form useful barrier settlements on the frontiers. . . . Thus they may become interested in the public welfare, and assist in promoting it; instead of being dangerous, as they now are, should any enemy promise them a better condition."[21]

The negotiating John Quincy Adams wrote to Secretary of State James Monroe during the War of 1812, telling him about the British plan to use its former Indian allies as a huge buffer state between the States and its own possessions in Canada. The area in question stretched from the Great Lakes to the Ohio River. On September 5, 1814, Adams wrote: "But when the boundary is once defined it is immaterial whether the Indians are upon it or not. Let it be a desert. . . ."[22] Sen. Stephen A. Douglas was so fearful that the famous Indian Barrier, an old buffer state on the western borders of Kansas, Missouri, and Iowa, would block the progress of Manifest Destiny, he was at pains to introduce the first bill to create the Territory of Nebraska.[23]

Frank Baum's description of the "Barrier of Invisibility" is a direct reference to what Americans called "the invisible barrier": the Canadian border. Henry David Thoreau called it so in 1850, in crossing the border at Rouses Point, New York.[24] Baum probably heard the expression in connection with the Fenian raids shortly after the Civil War. The notion of an invisible barrier could easily intrigue the childlike imagination. The Canadian border again came to his attention in Aberdeen, where this nearby eight-hundred–mile imaginary line had lately sheltered Sitting Bull.

The "Barrier of Invisibility" also refers to that "invisible barrier" that separated the mortal world from the realm of the supernatural called "Faerie." The Irish *immrama*—tales of sea voyages—recorded the adventures of sailors carried unknowingly across these barriers by storms, mist, raging wind. Baum's Shifting Sands may echo the *immrama's* descriptions of the shifting islands that filled the North Atlantic and the Irish Sea.

The geography of Dakota Territory itself appears in the Oz fantasy in the form of the marked separation of east and west. Dividing the territory in half was "the Big Road," the Missouri River. The two areas were called East River and West River.

The big difference is probably the simple fact that although South Dakota is a rural state the East River half has more towns, more schools, and easier access to Minneapolis, Sioux City, Des Moines, Omaha, and Lincoln, giving the people at least a slightly more cosmopolitan view of life and an easier acceptance of ideas and cultural trends coming from the East. Their language and speech patterns are midwestern, while those of West River are western. It is not quality that distinguishes East River from West River, nor even racial relationships, but rather the degree of isolation and the differences in social structure caused by differences of the land.[25]

The Emerald City is Frank Baum's tribute to the sudden sheer beauty of the Black Hills, rising from the desert desolation:

> The Black Hills are an oasis of verdure among the open and level plains. A luxuriant growth of grass spreads over the whole region; even on the rocky hillsides grass is found growing in the crevices in the rocks wherever there is a particle of soil for its support. A heavy forest covers the greater portion of this area, the trees growing thickly together and attaining full size, not only on the rich bottomlands of the valleys but on the tops of the level limestone "mesa"; and the steep rocky ridges are clothed with pine of good size to their very crests.[26]

In contrast to the desolation and the gloom, the Black Hills seemed almost like a mirage to the weary traveler. Close by, the Hills appear to be a deep green; from a distance of thirty miles, they are black; from fifty miles, they seem to be blue. The granite and limestone ranges are among the older of the world's mountains.

The ruby- and diamond-studded Emerald City reflects the mineral wealth of the Black Hills. For the white invaders, this was the main consideration: "When our population, swarming West, had reached the boundary of arable land, as if to stimulate our energy, on the face of the sterile waste, beyond, the land was suddenly in parts found covered with gold and silver, floored with coal. It was thought a fable." The potential wealth led Ralph Waldo Emerson to rhapsodize some more: "Here is *man* in the Garden of Eden; here is Genesis and the Exodus. . . . America is such a garden of plenty. . . ."[27]

The ensuing conflicts stemming from unrestrained greed, the assaults on the hills—faithfully recorded in Frank Baum's allegory—were no fable. But if the rude dispossession of the native American nations troubled Frank Baum, it was only to the extent that this land situation reminded him of another people unfairly treated, troubling him enough to create an Emerald City to represent the Emerald Isle: the beloved Ireland. The stubborn opposition to the domination of 8 million Irish by 8,000 landlords led to the "land war," which lasted for three years, beginning in 1879. During these years, Frank Baum was writing a series of Irish melodramas, including *The Maid of Arran*, which toured from New York to Canada, to Lincoln, Nebraska and all points between.[28]

Irish interest in forming independent farming colonies in the United States is a long one:

> . . . In 1817, the Irish Emigrant Society of New York petitioned Congress to set aside public lands in Illinois to which the Irish might repair before "the tempter . . . presents to their lips the cup that turns man to brute, and the very energies which would have made the fields to blossom make the city groan."
>
> . . . They asked Congress to sell land, on fourteen years' credit, to deserving Irishmen, who would serve as a frontier guard against wild Indians. After four hours of debate, the House of Representatives, by a vote of eighty-three to seventy-one, turned down the request—probably with serious consequences for the future of the Irish in America. Opposition to the measure came largely from southern members.[29]

Some of the projects proposed over the next several decades were actually schemes involving land speculation for simple profit, but many were genuinely altruistic concerns, such as

Fr. Jeremiah F. Trecy's attempt to establish the Saint Patrick's Colony in Nebraska in the 1850s. Then "in 1858, a letter from San Francisco printed in *The Irish News* of New York proposed forming a stock company in the East to purchase one of the states of Mexico and establish a republic where the green flag might fly over an independent Ireland. A letter to Secretary of State Steward, in 1863, recommended building a New Ireland somewhere in the western territories, with Thomas Francis Meagher, refugee of 1848 and Civil War soldier, as governor."[30]

Irish communities subsequently sprang up all over Minnesota, Nebraska, and Kansas. Gen. John O'Neill in 1872 decided "to build up a young Ireland on the virgin prairies of Nebraska and there rear a monument more lasting than granite or marble to the Irish race in America."[31] By 1882, the town of O'Neill was the county seat, and by 1891 it had 2,000 people—as many as Aberdeen, which was only 200 miles north. In the Dakota Territory itself, there were little isles of Erin at Limerick, or Brule city, and at Lalla Rookh, the pond near Yankton.

Frank Baum probably took special note of the career of one Charles Collins. Many Irish nationalists did. In the year 1869, Collins, with John Pope Hodnett, the United States assessor for Dakota Territory, plotted to establish a colony on the Missouri River. They hoped that well-armed and equipped Irish settlers would then be able to take advantage of "England's difficulty" and "Ireland's opportunity" when the time came for an assault on the British Northwest. On October 5, 1871, sixty Fenians rushed the Canadian border and actually captured a Hudson Bay Company post before being driven off by U.S. soldiers. The adventurers ended up in federal court. Charles Collins disappeared.

Collins's other dream in 1869 was to infiltrate the Black Hills, then under the "protection" of the Fort Laramie Treaty of 1868. Working for the Sioux City Iowa *Times*, Collins, the newsman, indubiously hastened the attack on the Hills by printing actual and fictional interviews with frontiersmen, trappers, and officers who had been there. He extolled the mineral wealth to be had for free and the goodness of "perpetuating careers like those of Daniel Boone and our other historical pioneers." Such tub thumping on American history soon bore practical results:

> The War Department, remembering off and on that the Black Hills belonged to the Sioux by treaty, attempted to discourage the first civilian expeditions, but failed. The first party was organized in Sioux City, Iowa, by Charles Collins and T. H. Russell, with Tom Gordon as captain. Leaving on October 6, and arriving near Sturgis on December 9, the party included Annie D. Tallent who, with her nine-year-old son, had decided to accompany her husband. As a result of her 350-mile trek she became known as "the first white woman in the Black Hills." (Twenty-five years later she was to write an early history of the area: *The Black Hills, or, The Last Hunting Ground of the Dakotahs*.) Hundreds of goldseekers followed during the next year.[32]

The Yellow Winkies are Frank Baum's allusion to the sizable Chinese population in the Old West. The word *Winkies* is a reference to the fact that white Americans seemed to believe that Chinese people were winking at them, as a result of the physical formation of the Oriental eyelid. The word *Winkie* is pejorative, because to those who were afraid of Oriental people, "the mere fold of an eyelid became a sign of sinister mystery and cunning, concealing more than it revealed; the 'slanty eyes' of chinese merchants, schoolteachers, garment workers, and marine corps sergeants became symbols of their devious, inscrutable, secretive, and evil minds."[33]

The fact that Frank Baum refers to the Winkies as slaves is significant, inasmuch as free white Americans in his day tended to associate the Chinese with slavery, even as the Chinese associated free white Americans with slavery also.[34] In the political allegory, the Yellow Winkies are gradually emancipated:

"Once was when she had made the Winkies her slaves, and set herself to rule over their country. . . . And then she called a dozen of her slaves, who were the Winkies, and gave them sharp spears, telling them to go to the strangers and destroy them. . . . But they could find no way to get out of the castle, for it was constantly guarded by the Yellow Winkies, who were the slaves of the Wicked Witch and too afraid of her not to do as she told them. There was great rejoicing among the Yellow Winkies, for they had been made to work hard during many years for the Wicked Witch, who had always treated them with great cruelty. . . . So they called the Yellow Winkies and asked them if they would help to rescue their friends, and the Winkies said they would be delighted to do all in their power for Dorothy, who had set them free from bondage."[35]

Free Chinese emigrants had indeed been "made to work hard," "with great cruelty," especially for the Central Pacific Railroad. The Irish worked for the Union Pacific, and the two lines met in the first transcontinental railroad at Promontory Point, Utah, in 1869. Feelings between the companies were not amiable, in general. *The Irish World and American Industrial Vindicator* demanded that the Chinese be deported because all slave labor had to be eradicated from the United States. The San Francisco *Alta California* observed in 1853 that the Chinese were "more clannish, therefore more dangerous than the negro, more cunning and deceitful" and so they were "less fitted to become menials and servants." Labor competition lay at the root of the strife, especially in mining. Many American get-rich-quick amatuers resented the superior skill of Chinese who had become professional miners in gold before leaving their native land.[36]

The Yellow Winkies are not the only reference that Baum makes to the Chinese in *The Wonderful Wizard of Oz*. Toward the end of his allegory, he describes creatures who are made entirely of china. The pun is an obvious one and natural to

Baum, who, for five years after leaving the Dakota Territory, was a traveling salesman in chinaware, going from farm to farm in the countryside around Chicago. There is a china princess in the allegory, which one critic has suggested represents the Chinese dowager empress Tzu Hsi, who had resisted foreign interference in her land. Writing in the summer of 1899, shortly before the Boxer Rebellion, Frank Baum may have expressed a slight contempt for her resistance by describing his princess as "fearful that a mended crack might mar her beauty, lives a lonely and isolated life, avoiding all contact with those who might chip her perfection."[37] Baum also describes this part of the Land of Oz as surrounded by a china wall. The Great Wall of China was built to keep out foreign invaders.

The Deadly Poppy Field is an impressively innocent, pretty symbol for opium. Opium and cocaine were sold on the free market during most of Baum's lifetime. Until 1913, citizens entered almost any pharmacy to buy these drugs at a reasonable price. Although opium was recognized as debilitating, it was still a matter of personal choice—not of political dictate—what drugs an individual could use. Opium especially was distributed in the form of patent medicines. It at least killed pain effectively, at a time when the country doctors themselves had few reliable cures that did not, it seemed to many, kill outright.

Baum pictures a great meadow of scarlet poppies and speaks of "the poison of the flowers." In these references, he alludes to the opium dream and the supposed death of addiction: "Now it is well known that when there are many of these flowers together their odor is so powerful that anyone who breathes it falls asleep, and if the sleeper is not carried away from the scent of the flowers he sleeps on and on forever. . . . If we leave her here she will die. . . . We must leave him here to sleep on forever, and perhaps he will dream that he has found courage at last."[38]

In the musical-extravaganza stage version of Baum's book, which opened in Chicago on June 16, 1902, brightly dressed chorus girls played the animated poppies. The audiences seldom failed to go berserk over the manic and melodramatic speech of the good witch Locasta, which that character delivers upon discovering that her favorites are in the "deadly grasp of these treacherous blossoms. . . . Heartless and poisonous flowers, dare you defy the power of the Witch of the North? Defy me, who rules the North Wind and holds the Frost King as a willing subject? For this you shall die. . . ."[39] This speech goes on in an extremely lurid manner. The crowds greeted it with "volleys of applause." The "curse" speech was a convention on the American stage, often delivered by a noble, dying Indian chief or a noble, dying black African prince. These stage creations cursed the white man for destroying their peoples. The curses were so popular because they provided white audiences with a painless way of expiating guilt, while continuing to profit by exploitation.[40]

The Wicked Witch of the West is a symbol that evokes the late Victorian fears of blacks, Indians, and women. When Baum was writing *The Wonderful Wizard of Oz* in 1899, Chicago was absorbing for the first time great numbers of black migrants from the South. The arrival of black women especially, to take jobs in the domestic service, brought to the fore previously repressed hostility from affluent whites.[41] There was a popular notion at the turn of the century that there was something evil or "wicked" about black women per se.

In describing the Wicked Witch of the West in her death as "melting away like brown sugar," Baum makes an allusion to black women. As if to stress his point, Baum repeats the color: ". . . the Witch fell down in a brown, melted, shapeless mass and began to spread over the clean boards of the kitchen floor." The original illustrations for the book reinforce this message: the witch has the distinctive hair style of the "pickaninny"—beribboned, braided pigtails sticking out in several directions.[42]

As a symbol, the Wicked Witch of the West derives much of its appeal from the traditional colonial American confounding of American Indians with European witches. The religiously driven English settlers, viewing the world as a great metaphysical battle between Good and Evil and as little else, were incapable of considering the native peoples simply as people. Indians could be comprehended only as degenerated members of the Ten Lost Tribes of Israel or as agents of the Black Man—the Devil. The woods were seen literally as the Devil's Bastion. From the zealous Puritan perspective, Indians and witches seemed identical in the same heretic light.[43]

The Virginia minister Alexander Whitaker in 1613 described the local medicine men thus: "Their Priests . . . are no other but such as our English Witches are. . . ." Priests were cohorts of the dreaded Pope; the first edition *New England Primer* frontispiece depicts the Vicar of Christ pierced by many arrows. More than two centuries later, Nathaniel Hawthorne deepens the moral brooding in "Young Goodman Brown" by relating how the young Puritan attends a witches' Sabbath in the woods, with "Indian priests and powwows, who had often scared their native forest with more hideous incantations than any known to English witchcraft."

Frank Baum's fable is the chronicle of a child's redemptive journey away from civilization, as represented by the harsh life on the Kansas prairie. Here is the innocent girl's dream, her search for secret and magical cures for her friends, her capture, adoption, and enslavement by an evil figure, and the killing of this evil one, followed by a triumphant return to civilization with redeeming knowledge and renewed health. In its essential elements and structure, the Oz allegory belongs to the already 200-year-old tradition of the Indian captivity narrative.

> For a century and a half before the first Leatherstocking tales, the public had feasted on the autobiographical abduction narrative, which under the color of personal history produced many of the pleasurable effects of fiction. The specimens of this type read by the Puritans ordinarily illustrated the power of the Lord to deliver the righteous from the imps of Satan, as the title of the earliest suggests—*The Soveraignty and Goodness of*

God, Together with the Faithfulness of His Promise Displayed; Being a Narrative of the Captivity and Restoration of Mrs. Mary Rowlandson (1682).[44]

For this minister's wife, captivity by the Wampanoags was the test sent by a just God for her "provoking sins," not the end result of acts by the Wampanoags. Her narrative is a religious confession, marked by allegorical thinking, simplicity, and direct detail. For her Puritan contemporaries, the journey itself assumed a religious import:

> When conceived of as the tale of a chosen people, the history of New Englanders naturally reminded the pious of the trials of the Israelites of old. Like the Old Testament Jews the Puritans fled a corrupt Egypt, in their case Anglican England, for the promised land, and like those ancient Israelites they too landed in the desert or wilderness, often spoken of as "howling" or "savage" and usually inhabited by Satan's agents. . . . The journey into the wilderness became as much a controlling metaphor for the story of the Puritans collectively as the spiritual pilgrimage formed the basis of the personal narrative, and the struggle between Puritans and Indians represented externally what the conflict between conscience and sin did internally. In fact, some modern commentators argue that the Puritans' image of the Indian was the projection of the fears and repressed desires in themselves upon the outsiders they encountered in America, and so the extermination of the Indian was part of the Puritan cleansing of sin from themselves. Others see such imagery as mere cant designed to justify Puritan expropriation of native lands.[45]

The genuine expression of religious sentiment in the Puritan captivity narratives gradually yielded to more secular expressions: the genre began to serve the public as a vehicle for propaganda and Indian hating. Cotton Mather thus fulminates against the "furious tawnies" and the "raging dragons" who had captured the famed Hannah Duston. Puritan brooding over sins gave way to the celebration of white retaliatory violence. Captives now escaped by their own guile, not by the grace of a beneficent Providence. The first fictionalized Indian captivity narrative appeared in 1799 with Charles Brockden Brown's *Edgar Huntly; or, Memoirs of a Sleep-Walker*. This secular trend culminated in the blood-and-thunder, lurid, and gory "dime novels" and the equally lurid popular tales in the medicine-show almanacs.

Despite the changes in the captivity narrative over several centuries of development, the basic core remained unchanged.[46] One scholar singles out the common themes: "The journey of the archtypal initiate, then, proceeds from Separation (abduction), Transformation (ordeal, accommodation, and adoption), and Return (escape, release, or redemption). This ritual passage, one of the most fundamental of all archtypal patterns, finds expression in the narratives of Indian captivity to an extent that renders this configuration an essential structuring device of the tales."*[47]

The Wonderful Wizard of Oz reflects this ritual pattern in other ways. The captivity narratives usually began with the Indian attack on the settler's house, the captive being led away with family and friends lying in their blood. Perhaps this is why it seems so satisfying that Dorothy is an orphan living with her aunt and uncle, is carried away violently by a cyclone, and falls on the Wicked Witch of the East, killing her. The Indian captivity narratives were the chronicles of the Christian experience of religious conversion, the death and rebirth of the spirit, and marked an attempt by the Puritans to resist the threat of "going native"—that is, of abandoning the white community in favor of the attractive Indian way of life. In the ritual, the resistance to this very real temptation is marked by the killing of the Indian captor. In Baum's political allegory, the child is unwilling to kill the Wicked Witch of the West,

*Richard Van Der Beets, "The Indian Captivity Narrative as Ritual" in AMERICAN LITERATURE 43:4 (January 1972), p. 562. Copyright © 1972 by the Duke University Press

but the wizard makes precisely this the one condition necessary for her return to Kansas.[48] The Wicked Witch of the West must die. Upon returning to Kansas, the child is asked where she has come from: " 'From the Land of Oz,' said Dorothy, gravely." Frank Baum uses the word *gravely*. In the land of dreams there is death and sorrow, terror, loss, and irrevocable moral compromise. The child is a child no more. She says, "I'm so glad to be at home again!"

The Wizard is the master of these ceremonies. This figure is based on the "pitchmen," as they were called, of the traveling Indian medicine shows. Pitchmen were also called "doctors," "professors,." "wizards," and "white witch doctors." Baum makes his Wizard a humble man from Omaha, Nebraska, who used to go up in balloons to draw crowds to the circus. In the Land of Oz, he plays the benevolent despot, never working genuine cures, but keeping the people happy with illusions, ruling behind the fearful mask of his reputation.

Medicine-show pitchmen—who were always white—were expected to deliver a solemn and impressive lecture, often presenting the only important fact about the medicine being sold—namely, the source of its recipe. This was the heart of the medicine-show ritual. The doctor would relate how he, the white man, had adventured long among, say, the Modocs or the Aztecs or the Incas, and at the greatest peril had wrested the secrets of their cures away. These secrets were then returned to civilization and patented as "nostrums"—a word that means "ours." These medicine-show pitch fables were based on old Indian captivity narratives. Proprietors of medicine-show companies often printed them in their paperbacks or almanacs, which, along with the Bible, were often the only literature in the settlers' homes.

In historical reality, the Indian had usually been most generous in aiding and curing the ailing whites on the frontiers. The "discovery" of the Indian use of quinine, or "the bark" or "Peruvian bark," convinced many that the Indian was indeed a healer with secrets. And right here is the vital, exonerating fantasy that the medicine shows lived on: that despite the theft of their land and livelihood, despite the arrogance and cruelty of the whites, the Indians still were interested in the health and welfare of their conquerors. Capon Springs water was a gift from the Catauba Indians.

The medicine shows, no matter what variety they were, the minstrel type, the Indian, or the "Quaker," all had three basic elements: the scare, the story, and the selling. The "rubes" and "natives" were first threatened with disease. Fear was stirred by the Indians rented from the nearby reservation, who "war-danced" and whooped to the incessant beating of the drums and the steady harangue and rant from the "doctor." At the crescendo of the frenzy, the bottles were distributed. The Indian doctor, browbeating his marks, resembled the medieval priest, driving his peasants into buying indulgences for their sins. The settlers came to get the alcohol and the opium in the nostrums to kill their physical aches and pains. The drama provided them with psychic relief. In short, the pitchmen were experts in relieving the citizens of their pain, their guilt, and their cash.

The sources of Frank Baum's allegorical symbol of the Wizard lie deep in terror, directed by white political leaders and private citizens against the Indian nations for centuries. John Collier said that "beginning about 1870, a leading aim of the United States was to destroy the Plains Indians' societies through destroying their religions; and it may be that the world has never witnessed a religious persecution so implacable and so variously implemented."[49] The white attack centered on the Indian medicine men. To his people, the medicine man was a leader—moral exemplar, historian, philosopher, warrior, friend, teacher, healer. More than anyone else, the medicine man knew that the white man's rum, whiskey, and disease were poison for his people. "As one of the strongest unifying factors in any Indian community, the Indian medicine man became the object of the most intense hatred of Europeans striving to weaken and dominate his tribe. Vogel remarks that 'all of the principal forces of European erosion of Indian society have been brought to bear in the assault against the medicine man. To the extent that his influence was weakened, white influence was able to penetrate.' "[50]

Perhaps the most duplicitous and insidious attack came from white Christian missionaries. The missionaries despised the medicine man not only on political, racial, and religious grounds, but also for his often superior medical skill. Daniel Gookin, in charge of the Christian Indian settlements for the United Colonies in the 1680s, considered the powwows to be nothing but witches and wizards having a familiarity with Satan. John Eliot deliberately showed Indians the general principles of physic and the anatomy of man's body in hopes that they would no longer fear leaving their own medicine men. ". . . by this means we should train up these poor Indians in that skill which would confound and root out their powwows. . . ." This malice of the Christian ministers was so great that most white settlers would adopt Indian herbal cures with great fear only and contrition, after being informed that the medicine men were drawing their pharmaceutical knowledge from the Black Man. Over the centuries, white settlers built up huge reservoirs of guilt and ill feeling over the Indian medicine men, which could be easily, and profitably, tapped by the white wizards of the traveling Indian medicine shows.

Frank Baum had a deep interest in these shows. With his early interest in and knowledge of the Pennsylvania oil country, he was aware that oil was used primarily as medicine before the discovery of its use for light and lubrication.[51] He had been a traveling salesman both in chinaware and for his family's oil-product retail store in New York. The medicine shows were immensely popular entertainment and so appealed to the playwright and actor in Baum. And finally, his congenitally weak heart, which had caused him to abandon traveling sales, led Baum to hope for health and perhaps to some necessity to believe in a wonderful wizard.

The Wizard of Oz, ruling his empire anonymously behind the Barrier of Invisibility in 1899, very clearly and forcibly suggests the 1869 Imperial Wizard of the Invisible Empire of the South, the Ku Klux Klan. In the year 1869, Baum was a daydreaming thirteen-year-old with a lively imagination. The Klan exploitation of European legendry and mythology for its own purposes of mystification and terror must have bewildered and also appealed to Frank Baum—as it did everyone else. Possibly the child turned again to literalism in order to deal with the puzzle, wondering who or what would live in an invisible empire. Indeed, the Ku Klux Klan may well have been the genesis of the Oz allegory.[52] What is clear is that the Civil War and black slavery were of immense concern to the child, who had experienced both firsthand: the words *slavery* and *bondage* appear more than twenty times in *The Wonderful Wizard of Oz*. The close approach of Gen. Robert E. Lee to the Pennsylvania oil fields and New York in 1863, on his way to Gettysburg, could not have failed to have alarmed Frank Baum, then seven years old.

The establishment of legal status for segregation in the United States was a gradual process, beginning after the Civil War and virtually complete by the turn of the century. The expressions for those situations were "Jim Crow" and "lynch law." Frank Baum wrote "Bandit Jim Crow," one of his intensely moralistic tales in the 1890s. In *The Wonderful Wizard of Oz*, in an almost parablelike passage, Baum introduces the essential emotional elements involved in segregation, in describing the relationship of the Scarecrow to the crows. These include the "scare," or fear, involved, the self-doubts about one's worth, the sense of desertion and abandonment, the false pride, and the deception. In the dialogue between the old crow passing by and the Scarecrow, Frank Baum seems to be suggesting, through his satire, that the man who makes himself feel important by scaring crows is not really a man, but only something stuffed with straw. But the satire is diffuse.[53] This may not be his intent.

In the year immediately following the huge success of *The Wonderful Wizard of Oz*, Baum wrote and published a fantasy titled *The Life and Adventures of Santa Claus*. It is apparent that his frontier experiences were still on his mind. The book was illustrated by Mary Cowles Clark—tomahawks, spears, the traditional hide-covered teepees, and the faces of obviously Indian men, women, children, and papooses fill the pages and their margins. Baum describes the "rude tent of skins on a broad plain." Two crucial chapters are titled "The Wickedness of the Awgwas" and "The Great Battle Between Good and Evil." The Awgwas seem to be a representation of native Americans: "that terrible race of creatures" and "the wicked tribe." Baum condemns the Awgwas and in the process seems to forget momentarily that children's vocabularies are limited: "You are a transient race, passing from life into noth-ingness. We, who live forever, pity but despise you. On earth you are scorned by all, and in Heaven you have no place! Even the mortals, after their earth life, enter another exist-ence for all time, and so are your superiors."[54] Predictably enough, a few pages later, "all that remained of the wicked Awgwas was a great number of earthen hillocks dotting the plain."[55]

Significantly allied to the Awgwas in these two chapters are other races: "There were three hundred Asiatic Dragons, breathing fire that consumed everything it touched. These hated mankind and all good spirits. And there were the three-eyed Giants of Tatary, a host in themselves, who liked nothing better than to fight. And next came the Black Demons from Patalonia. . . ."[56] Baum also describes "the Forest of Ethop"—an obvious allusion to Ethiopia—"the wild jungle of an unknown land."

Frank Baum considered himself the historian of his fan-tasy empire, and it is in this role that he speaks at the opening and the close of these two chapters:

> I do not like to mention the Awgwas, but they are a part of this history, and can not be ignored. . . .
> Now I will gladly have done with wicked spirits and with fighting and bloodshed. It was not from choice that I told of the Awgwas and their allies, and of their great battle with the immortals. They were part of this history, and could not be avoided.[57]

Future generations of historians in the United States did ig-
nore the racial aspects of Baum's work, in the interests of
sloughing off that which conscience could not assimilate.

> . . . how acutely popular writers sensed the cross-cur-
> rents in American society remains unclear; there is no
> question, however, that they implicitly sustained the
> conservative position of the ruling order. . . .
> The nineteenth-century romances of the frontier,
> while not entirely free of subversive elements, mine
> western legendry within the context of progressivism;
> in nearly every instance virtue is rewarded, honesty vin-
> dicated, and Manifest Destiny justified, whatever the
> cost to art and probability. Yet, these ostensibly innocent
> novels, concluding with pious progressive chords, subtly
> invoke notes of the primitive during the journey through
> the wilderness and obliquely betray cleavages in the
> American mind.[58]

Notes

1. Frank Joslyn Baum and Russell P. MacFall, *To Please A Child; A Biography of L. Frank Baum, Royal Historian of Oz*. (Chicago: Reilly and
Lee, 1961), p. 236.
2. Lyman Frank Baum, *The Wizard of Oz*, with pictures of W. W. Denslow
(New York: Rand McNally and Co., paperback edition, 1956). This introduction seems distantly to echo, in Baum's unsophisticated way, Charles
Brockden Brown's famous statement of literary intent by way of preface to
the popular novel *Edgar Huntly; or, Memoirs of a Sleep-Walker* (1799). In
describing the then-frontier country of eastern Pennsylvania, Brown was
the first American writer to fictionalize the popular Indian captivity narratives. Growing up in nearby Chittenango, New York, Baum may well
have read Brockden Brown as he was a local writer.
3. In the interests of avoiding responsibility, Baum refused to recognize
his own work as specifically political allegory. He insisted on obscurantism,
ever associating his work with "folklore, legends, myths and fairy tales"—which
are all born of centuries-old oral traditions, not individual effort. Only an
individual can be held responsible for an allegory. Baum had excellent
reasons for calling his work a "modernized fairy tale" and for avoiding
"allegory."

4. Anthony F. C. Wallace, *The Death and Rebirth of the Seneca*, with the assistance of Sheila C. Steen. (New York: Alfred A. Knopf, Inc., 1970), p. 185.

5. There is a picture of Lyman Frank Baum on the souvenir cover for his Irish melodrama—in which he also starred—*The Maid of Arran*. The twenty-six–year–old had probably written the words accompanying this picture in 1882: "A Souvenir Of The Maid of Arran—An Idyllic Irish Drama Written For The People, Irrespective Of Caste Or Nationality—A Play To Ensnare All Hearts And Leave An Impress Of Beauty And Nobility Within The Sordid Mind of Man."

6. Benjamin Baum may have told his son the old European peasant belief that whirlwinds contain witches and wizards. His ancestors came from the Palatinate, an area spanning both sides of the Rhine, around Heidelberg and Mannheim. Also, in the summer of 1899, when Baum was writing his fantasy in Chicago, Carrie A. Nation began her saloon-smashing career, or "hatchetation," in Medicine Hat, Kansas. That she earned the sobriquet Cyclone Carrie or the Kansas Cyclone may not be entirely unrelated to the work of Frank Baum.

7. *The Complete Tales of Washington Irving*, edited and with an introduction by Charles Neider (Garden City, New York: Doubleday and Company, Inc., 1975), p. 15, cited from Irving's postscript to his story. Henry Hudson was set adrift in 1611 by mutineers, with eight loyal crew members. In "Rip Van Winkle," this lost crew of the *Half-Moon* plays ninepins in a hollow of the mountain, Irving describing their old Dutch dress, with high-rolled boots, doublets, and high-crowned hats. In the Denslow illustrations for *The Wonderful Wizard of Oz*, the Munchkins seem very like the old Dutch settlers in New York, though Baum's "little people" may well have been inspired more by his mother's tales of the Irish leprechauns, gnomes, elves, sprites, dryads, pixies, and dwarfs.

8. *The Annotated Wizard of Oz: The Wonderful Wizard of Oz by Lyman Frank Baum*, with introduction, notes, and bibliography by Michael Patrick Hearn (New York: Clarkson N. Potter, Inc./Publisher, 1973), p. 19. Hearn adores Baum. The comedy "Our Landlady" column for December 6, 1890, probably written with the good intention of easing white settlers' fears over the Ghost Dance, also illustrates Baum's implicit callousness. It is titled "She Talks to Hole-in-the-Face And Gets A Story." The "comical" name of the fictional Indian in the title is an allusion to two Indians well known to Baum's neighbors, Rain-in-the-Face, and Rift-in-the-Clouds, the latter known to whites by a bad translation as Hole-in-the-Day. Interested in finding something ludicrous to laugh at, Baum disregarded or never learned that the name Rain-in-the-Face signified courage in the face of adversity and that Rift-in-the-Clouds was so named because at his birth, the sun burst forth and lifted the mother's sadness over the father's recent death. The famous hereditary chief and peacemaker called Young-Man-Afraid-of-His-

Horses became in Baum's fiction, Young-Man-Afraid-of-His-Pocketbook. Such juvenile humor is repulsive in any man who has reached the age of discretion and indicates the presence of more dangerous attitudes. (The original source is L. Frank Baum's "Our Landlady;" Midwestern life in the Nineties as seen and recorded by the author of the "Oz" books in a weekly newspaper column unearthed and transcribed by members of the South Dakota Writers' Project, Work Projects Administration, Sponsored by Friends of the Middle Border, 1941), pp. 37–39.

9. Col. D. S. Stanley (later brigadier general) was Custer's superior officer on a railroad survey expedition. Cited from a letter to his wife in Ralph K. Andrist's *The Long Death* (New York: Macmillan, 1964).

10. Eva Katharine Gibson, *Zauberlinda; or, The Wise Witch* (Chicago: Robert Smith Printing Company, 1902).

11. During Red Cloud's War (1866–68), Frank Baum was a cadet attending Peekskill Military Academy. His mother had sent him there in the hopes of curing his daydreaming. The young and confirmed pacifist did not enjoy the atmosphere. Cadet Baum is not likely to have imbibed tolerant views of the Indians while at this particular institute of higher learning.

12. Growing up in Chittenango, New York, Baum must have been deeply impressed by the repeated nearby assaults by Irish Fenians across the Canadian border. Almost 100,000 Fenian sympathizers had demonstrated in March 1866 in Jones' Wood, New York, to raise $50,000. Two months later, on June 1, 1866, 800 men, led by John O'Neill, a former cavalry officer in the Union army, attacked and captured Fort Erie, the Canadian settlement across the border from Buffalo. With 8 dead and 20 wounded, but with 3,000 more men waiting to join in, the American losses would have been far more severe but for the timely intervention of the USS *Michigan*, which blocked the reinforcements and their supplies.

13. In calling the British "monkeys," Baum is bitterly turning the tables on those Americans of the middle classes who were fond of regarding both blacks and immigrant Irish as apelike. The political cartoons of the period are filled with depictions of Irish in simian aspects.

14. R. S. Macbeth, M.A., *Policing the Plains; Being the Real-Life Record of the Famous Royal North-West Mounted Police* (London: Hodder and Stoughton, Ltd., 1922), p. 27.

15. Hugh Alymer Dempsey, *Crowfoot; Chief of the Blackfeet*, with a foreword by Paul F. Sharp (Norman, Oklahoma: The University of Oklahoma Press, 1972), p. 115.

16. Henry M. Littlefield, "The Wizard of Oz: Parable on Populism," (*The American Quarterly*, published by the University of Pennsylvania, 16 (Spring 1964) No. 1: p. 55. Copyright 1964, Trustees of the University of Pennsylvania. In this passage cited by Littlefield, Baum seems to be aware of the historical migration of several Indian tribes from the forest and the lake country to the Great Plains.

17. Early American travelers mentioned "The Great Sandy Desert," but it was the famed explorer Stephen H. Long who named it the Great American Desert in 1821. Three years later, the region was first labelled as such in a geography textbook. And as late as 1851, Herman Melville would preface some advice to his readers with "Should you ever be athirst in the great American desert" —referring, characteristically, to a spiritual desert.

18. James Fenimore Cooper, *The Pathfinder; or, The Inland Sea*, with an afterword by Thomas Berger (New York: The New American Library, Inc., 1961). Cooper wrote *The Pathfinder* in 1840.

19. Nowhere is the political significance of the myth of the great American desert better illustrated. The weather was indeed appalling, but life could be supported and with some beauty. The wind-blown sand, loosened from the underlying sandy bedrock, formed dunes that supported native grasses. There were miles of crisp buffalo grass or silvery sage, prickly white poppies, and blazing wild sunflowers, which sometimes overwhelmed the occasional sod shanty. Land speculation—always of interest to nineteenth-century politicians—was deeply affected by how the populace back east regarded the prairies.

20. Nathaniel Bartlett Sylvester, *Historical Sketches of Northern New York at the Adirondack Wilderness: Including Traditions of the Indians, Early Explorers, Pioneer Settlers, Hermit Hunters, etc.* (New York, 1877), pp. 283–84.

21. *The Complete Writings of Thomas Paine*, edited by Philip S. Foner (Secaucus, New Jersey: Citadel Press, 1945), 2: 303–33.

22. Virgil J. Vogel (ed.), *This Country Was Ours: A Documentary History of the American Indian*, with a foreword by Sol Tax (New York: Harper and Row, Publishers, 1972), pp. 79–81. The letter is cited from *Writings of John Quincy Adams*, 12 vols., edited by Worthington Chauncy Ford (New York: The Macmillan Co., 1915), 5: 110–21.

23. Ibid., pp. 142–44. Douglas is cited from a letter dated Washington, December 17, 1853, published in the Saint Joseph *Gazette*, March 15, 1854.

24. Henry David Thoreau, *A Yankee in Canada* (New York: Greenwood Press, 1969).

25. Herbert S. Schell, *History of South Dakota* (Lincoln, Nebraska: University of Nebraska Press, 1975), pp. 141–42. The meaning in the final sentence here is obscure.

26. Alexander B. Adams, *Sitting Bull: An Epic of the Plains* (New York: Putnam Sons, 1973), p. 263.

27. Stan Steiner, *The Vanishing White Man* (New York: Harper and Row, Publishers, 1976), p. 197. Steiner discusses the tendency of white exploiters to romanticize the land, especially with florid rhetoric.

28. Michael Davitt, later to be called the Father of the Land League, came to the United States in 1878 for an extensive lecture tour. Charles Stewart

Parnell, president of the Irish National Land League, came to the United States in the famine year of 1880 to raise funds to save tenant farmers from starvation and to unite people for agrarian reform.

29. Carl Witte, *The Irish in America* (New York: Russell and Russell, 1970), p. 63.

30. Ibid., p.66.

31. Ibid., p. 71.

32. John R. Milton, *South Dakota: A History* (New York: W. W. Norton and Company, Inc., 1977),p. 25.

33. Stan Steiner, *Fusang: The Chinese Who Built America* (New York: Harper and Row, Publishers, 1979), p. 212.

34. American business representatives in the Orient felt constrained to reassure prospective emigrants that they would not be cast into the lot of the black man in the United States. The broadsides issued in 1862 in Hong Kong, announcing that miners were needed in Oregon stated specifically that "There is no fear of slavery. All is nice" (Steiner, *Fusang*, note 33, pp. 113–14). The Chinese wondered who would win the Civil War.

35. Baum, *The Wizard of Oz*, pp. 139, 140, 147, 153, 154.

36. The terror was clear enough. During one night in 1871 in Los Angeles, white mobs lynched or burned alive twenty Chinese. In Rock Springs, Wyoming, in 1885, twenty-eight Chinese men were murdered, some again burned alive, with other torture as well.

37. Russel B. Nye, *The Wonderful Wizard of Oz and Who He Was* (East Lansing, Michigan: Michigan State University Press, 1957), cited in Hearn (ed.), *The Annotated Wizard of Oz*, p. 311.

38. Baum, *The Wizard of Oz*, pp. 87, 88, 89.

39. Baum and MacFall, *To Please a Child*, pp. 3–4.

40. White Americans tended to blame opium on the Chinese and their supposedly morally debilitated "opium dens." It was conveniently forgotten that it was England that had forced opium on China after "winning" the Opium Wars of 1839–44 and 1856–60. England forced the opening of four Chinese ports to opium brought in from India as payment for the tea taken away to satisfy the English addiction. Before the wars, opium had been strictly outlawed in China. It was especially ironic that Americans should blame opium on China, when their own national prosperity had been built on a drug called rum, forced on African nations for slaves.

41. The Baum family kept a black maid/cook in Chicago.

42. Black people were usually depicted so in books for white children. The year 1899 also saw the publication of *Little Black Sambo*, written by a white Englishwoman while riding a train to India.

43. This Puritan aspect of mind is discussed in the following:

> 1. Axtell, James. *The European and the Indian: Essays in the Ethnohistory of Colonial North America*. New York and Oxford: Oxford University Press, 1981.

2. Berkhofer, Robert F., Jr. *The White Man's Indian: Images of the American Indian from Columbus to the Present*. New York: Vintage Books, 1978.

3. Forbes, Jack D. (ed.). *The Indian in America's Past*. Englewood Cliffs, New Jersey: Prentice-Hall, Inc., 1964.

4. Pearce, Roy Harvey. *Savagism and Civilization: A Study of the Indian and the American Mind*. Baltimo.'e and London: The John Hopkins Press, 1953.

5. Segal, Charles M., and David C. Stineback. *Puritans, Indians, and Manifest Destiny*. New York: G. P. Putnam's Sons, 1977.

44. Arthur K. Moore, *The Frontier Mind: A Cultural Analysis of the Kentucky Frontiersman* (Lexington, Kentucky: University of Kentucky Press, 1957), p. 167.

45. Berkhofer, *The White Man's Indian*, pp. 82–83.

46. John Bunyan's *Pilgrim's Progress*, the English religious allegory that had the greatest influence on the course of American literature, has also the original dream, the journey or pilgrimage, and the happy home.

47. Richard Van Der Beets, "The Indian Captivity Narrative as Ritual," *American Literature*, 43 (January 1972), No. 4: 562.

48. In the most celebrated captivity narrative of all, that of Hannah Duston, the woman murders several Indian men in their sleep. Cotton Mather lauded this desperate woman; Nathaniel Hawthorne damned her as a "bloody hag." The ritual act of murder is present in American literature long before Lyman Frank Baum's allegory. In James Fenimore Cooper's *The Pathfinder* (1840):

> The dramatic turning point in the novel is reached when Deerslayer kills a man for the first time, in defense of the Hutter family. He has wished to avoid conflict but he has to keep the canoe, the key to the safety of the family on the lake, out of the hands of the attacking Indians. This act of social commitment forces him to kill the Indian who threatens to capture the canoe. It is his dying victim who tells him he has lost his innocence. Deerslayer, he says, "That good name for boy—poor name for warrior . . . eye sartain—finger lightning—aim, death—great warrior soon. No Deerslayer —Hawkeye—Hawkeye—Hawkeye." [David W. Noble, *The Eternal Adam and The New World Garden: The Central Myth in the American Novel Since 1830* (New York: Grossett and Dunlap, 1968), pp. 11–12).]

49. Forbes, *The Indian in America's Past*, p. 112.

50. Francis Jennings, *The Invasion of America: Indians, Colonialism, and the Cant of Conquest* (Chapel Hill, North Carolina: University of North Carolina Press, 1975), pp. 52–53. Virgil J. Vogel is cited from *American Indian Medicine*, XCV, Civilization of the American Indian Series (Norman,

Oklahoma: University of Oklahoma Press, 1970), Chapter 2.

51. On the banks of Oil Creek, the Seneca had dug pits and lined them with timber, into which the river water seeped. The oil was skimmed off the top with paddles. "David Zeisberger, the Moravian missionary who made a daring journey by the Forbidden Path through Seneca country to the headwaters of the Allegheny River, heard of various oil wells in the area. Of one in particular, which some members of his party visited in the vicinity of present Tionesta, he reported on October 7, 1768: 'They brought back some oil from the oil-well. . . . The Indians use it externally as a medicine and it would be possible to use it for lighting. . . . The nature of these oil-wells might well be investigated.' " (Paul A. W. Wallace, *Pennsylvania: Seed of a Nation*, [New York: Harper and Row, 1962], p. 222).

The Seneca used ointment for toothache, headache, swellings, rheumatism, sprains, burns. Sometimes they took the liniment internally. It was excellent also mixed with war paint. Early white settlers imitated the Indians in dipping blankets in the springs to collect the oil, especially in dry seasons when the water was low. They called it fossil oil, Genesee bank oil, American rock oil, and Barbadoes tar. The most common names were Seneca Oil, Indian Oil, and Snake Oil. The settlers mixed it with flour for axle grease and swallowed it "to purify the blood." Eventually one Samuel Kier bottled it as a patent medicine and made his fortune.

52. The prominent American literary historian Edward Wagenknecht once wrote about Lyman Frank Baum: "He was not, so far as I know, a member of the Ku Klux Klan." (*Utopia Americana*. [Seattle: University of Washington Chapbooks No. 28, University of Washington Bookstore, 1929], p. 23.) Wagenknecht does not elaborate here. Apparently there were people who thought that Baum had been a member at some time. Clearly there is room for more research here; the answer may well be lost to history. There were Klanlike organizations in the Pennsylvania oil fields, such as the "members of the new Oil Men's League, a secret society modeled on the Ku Klux Klan, with passwords and fiery symbols" (Jules Abels, *The Rockefeller Billions: The Story of the World's Most Stupendous Fortune*, [New York: the Macmillan Company, 1965], p. 79). The prominent social historian Ida Minerva Tarbell describes the resentment of the Standard Oil monopoly: ". . . Crowds gathered about the offices of the Standard threatening and jeering. Mysterious things, crossbones and death-heads were found plentifully sprinkled on the buildings owned by Standard. More than once the slumber of the oil towns was disturbed by marching bodies of men. It was certain that a species of Kuklux had hold of the Bradford regions and that a very little spark was needed to touch off the United Pipe Lines." (Abels, *The Rockefeller Billions*, p. 138.) As a reporter for the Bradford *Era*, Baum at least knew about these events. Men marched in white robes in 1872 and again in 1878.

53. The Wicked Witch of the West sends the King Crow to peck out the eyes of the strangers and tear them to pieces. The Tin Woodman responds

by catching forty crows by the head and twisting their necks until they die. Whatever this may mean allegorically, Frank Baum is dealing with the frontier experiences of violence and death. The Scarecrow sings, "Tol-de-ri-de-oh" as he walks along. This is a direct allusion to the European nursery rhyme "The carrion crow" sat upon an oak,/ And spied a taylor cutting out a cloak;/ With a heigh ho! the carrion crow!/ Sing tol de rol, de riddle row!" The pioneers forging west in covered wagons sang this ancient rhyme in ritual incantation, upon sighting trailside graves, abandoned possessions, or the "carrion crow" himself—the patient vulture. Buffalo bones lay on the prairie at the limits of Aberdeen. The Crow is Frank Baum's symbol for Jim Crow and the pioneer's experience of death. But it may also be another instance of comic literalism: the attack by the King Crow represents the threat of an "uprising" by warriors of the Crow nation.

54. Lyman Frank Baum, *The Life and Adventures of Santa Claus* (second printing, 1902; reprint, New York: Dover Publications, Inc., 1976), pp. 110–11.

55. A possible description of the Wounded Knee site, which Baum may have visited while living in Aberdeen.

56. Baum, *The Life and Adventures of Santa Claus*, p. 114.

57. Ibid., pp. 95, 119.

58. Moore, *The Frontier Mind*, pp. 184–85. The dislocations that Moore decries are, one suspects, utterly *irreconcilable*. In his great romance of the sea, *Moby Dick*, Herman Melville witnesses the American spiritual ship of state: ". . . then the rushing *Pequod*, freighted with savages, and laden with fire, and burning a corpse, and plunging into that blackness of darkness, seemed the material counterpart of her monomaniac commander's soul."

2

Nathaniel Hawthorne's House of the Seven Gables

Men must endure
Their going hence, even as their coming hither;
Ripeness is all.
                                        —*King Lear*

In writing *The House of the Seven Gables*, Nathaniel Hawthorne chose to tell a New England version of the legend of The Sleeping Beauty, or Little Briar-Rose. The brothers Jakob and Wilhelm Grimm were only twenty years older than Hawthorne and had collected their household tales in Germany when the American writer was still a child. "The Sleeping Beauty" first became popular in America at midcentury, and Hawthorne structured his romance on this enduring fable. He states clearly that "it is a Legend prolonging itself, from an epoch now gray in the distance, down into our own broad daylight, and bringing along with it some of its legendary mist. . . ."[1] The choice of the word *prolonging* indicates the story antecedent to *The House of the Seven Gables*.

Hawthorne was committed to children's literature. Early reading in Salem and the formal schooling at Bowdoin—where translating Virgil's *Aeneid* from the Latin was an entrance requirement—grounded Hawthorne in the classic legends of Greece and those of medieval Europe. For his children's stories, he rewrote the classic tales to conform to modern manners, customs, and morals—often with a strong historical theme. These old tales were "to be taken out of the cold moonshine of classical mythology, and modernized, or perhaps gothicized, so that they may be felt by children of these days."[2] This obscure man of letters, suffering the neglect of his more ambitious works, must have been deeply consoled by the success of his children's stories. On March 21, 1838, he wrote to Henry Wadsworth Longfellow describing his wish to "entirely revolutionize the whole system of juvenile literature."*[3] By midcentury, a less reform-minded Hawthorne, more relaxed and confident in familiar abilities, adapted "The Sleeping Beauty" to New England. Remaining true to the timeless themes of the medieval legend, while drawing a convincing portrait of modern life, was his challenge.

Hawthorne describes the House of the Seven Gables—architecturally, historically, and metaphysically—making it a setting proper for the "Legend prolonging itself": a castle. His romance is filled with references to castles. The mansion is "the scene of events more full of human interest, perhaps, than those of a gray, feudal castle. . . ." The land around the House of the Seven Gables yet remaining to the Pyncheons is called "the small desmesne"—an expression that usually signifies the land surrounding a medieval manor. Gervayse Pyncheon has known a "long abode in foreign parts, moreover, and familiarity with many of the castles and ancestral halls of England, and the marble palaces of Italy. . . ." In poverty, Hepzibah dreams of "castles in the air" and imagines an unexpected invitation to a "Pyncheon Hall." Hawthorne extends a metaphor of Judge Jaffrey Pyncheon's character as a magnificent palace.[4]

In both "The Sleeping Beauty" and *The House of the Seven Gables*, royal and aristocratic families are in eclipse, so Hawthorne refers frequently to titled people. Uncle Venner recalls that "in my young days, the great man of the town was called King, and his wife—not Queen, to be sure—but Lady." Passengers with Clifford Pyncheon on the railroad "had plunged into the English scenery and adventures of pamphlet-

*Quoted by permission of the Houghton Library.

36

novels, and were keeping company with dukes and earls." Gervayse Pyncheon hopes that his property will enable him to solicit an earldom and that his daughter, "the beautiful Alice Pyncheon, with the rich dowry which he could then bestow, might wed an English duke, or a German reigning-prince. . . ." A portrait of Alice is said to be with "the present Duke of Devonshire, and to be now preserved at Chatsworth. . . ."[5]

"The Sleeping Beauty" opens on a world of promise and prophecy, beauty, happiness, and festivity; then come a sudden betrayal, more prophecy, a curse, and the fulfillment of that curse. A beautiful daughter is born to the king, who orders a great feast to celebrate.[6] In the land there are thirteen wise women, but the king invites only twelve, because he has but twelve golden plates. During the feast, the wise woman who has been rejected solely for the sake of convenience enters and casts a curse, that the princess will prick her finger on the spindle of a loom on her fifteenth birthday and will fall down dead. The last wise woman to bestow her gift can only change this death curse to a deep sleep of 100 years.

Hawthorne knew that "wise woman" was medieval parlance for "witch." Aware also that his great-grandfather Judge John Hathorne had presided over the Salem witch trials in 1692, he made his character Matthew Maule a wizard condemned by Colonel Pyncheon. Like the rejected wise woman in "The Sleeping Beauty," Maule curses Pyncheon: "At the moment of execution—with the halter about his neck, and while Colonel Pyncheon sat on horseback, grimly gazing at the scene—Maule had addressed him from the scaffold, and uttered a prophecy of which history, as well as fireside tradition, has preserved the exact words—'God,' said the dying man . . . 'God will give him blood to drink!' "[7] This curse is fulfilled in succeeding generations, beginning with Colonel Pyncheon, who dies at his own feast to celebrate the opening of the House of the Seven Gables.[8]

Not to put too fine a point on it—for Hawthorne never did—the American curse is property. There is an element of economic exploitation introduced into *The House of the Seven Gables* which is not in the original legend. The curse falls on the king for simply failing to recognize the wise woman; lacking a golden plate is merely his excuse. But the Pyncheon family curse falls because of "ill-gotten gold, or real estate," as Clifford realizes: "What we call real estate—the solid ground to build a house on—is the broad foundation on which nearly all the guilt of this world rests. A man will commit almost any wrong—he will heap up an immense pile of wickedness, as hard as granite, and which will weigh as heavily upon his soul, to eternal ages—only to build a great, gloomy, dark-chambered mansion, for himself to die in, and for his posterity to be miserable in."[9] This is the perennial Pyncheon doubt about moral right to the property. Hawthorne insists: "If so, we are left to dispose of the awful query, whether each inheritor of the property—conscious of wrong, and failing to rectify it—did not commit anew the great guilt of his ancestor, and incur all its original responsibilities."[10]

The curse in *The House of the Seven Gables* takes the form of a relentless cycle of Pyncheon exploitation and arrogance, which yields an equally reprehensible Maule revenge by psychic violence. After two hundred years of this American feud, the Maules are believed to be extinct. The rich Jaffrey Pyncheon now preys on the poor side of his own family—the inevitable end of revenge. One simply expressed truth in "The Sleeping Beauty" is that a wrong act and its guilt leads without fail to a deep sleep or to the loss of love and affection. Only after a long and frequently bitter apprenticeship in exploring lost and submerged emotion—conducted in a country that all but completely denied the reality of individualized feeling—was Hawthorne able to accept this truth and be free to write well about sleep.

To present a sleep of 100 years convincingly in modern times, Hawthorne associates two Pyncheon women living precisely 100 years apart: Alice and Phoebe.

> . . . Hepzibah talked rather vaguely, and at great length, about a certain Alice Pyncheon, who had been exceed-

ingly beautiful and accomplished, in her lifetime, a
hundred years ago. The fragrance of her rich and de-
lightful character still lingered about the place where she
had lived, as a dried rosebud scents the drawer where
it has withered and perished. This lovely Alice had met
with some great and mysterious calamity, and had grown
thin and white, and gradually faded out of the world.
But, even now, she was supposed to haunt the House
of the Seven Gables. . . .[11]

In the Sleeping Beauty legend, the king is not at home
on his daughter's fifteenth birthday. The princess is quite
alone in the palace. In Hawthorne's modernization, Gervayse
Pyncheon is likewise not there for his daughter, Alice. Overwhelmed by greed, Gervayse fails to help Alice fend off the
machinations of the wizard Matthew Maule. He "had mar-
tyred his poor child to an inordinate desire for measuring his
land by miles, instead of acres." The father allows Maule to
mesmerize Alice—to enchant her—in hopes of finding the
missing document, the parchment key to the lost Pyncheon
legacy. But the savage Matthew seeks only revenge, and Gervayse discovers only the broken spirit of his daughter. Too
late, he cries, "Alice! Awake! . . . it troubles me to see you
thus! Awake!" But "Alice awoke out of her enchanted sleep"
only to waste away and die.[12] The fireside tradition in the
House of the Seven Gables tells how the sunny Alice had
played a gently melancholy harpsichord and how once in frolic
she had tossed into the air a handful of seeds from Italy, which
settled on one of the gables, to sprout and to become known
eventually as Alice's posies. This is the way it was with Alice
Pyncheon.
The accomplished beauty of modern times is Phoebe
Pyncheon. She is cheerful, sings lightly sad songs, and busily
tends the flowers and vegetables in the Pyncheon garden.
Here the artist Holgrave reads to Phoebe his version of the
Alice legend. Holgrave sees, upon finishing near sundown,
that he has unexpectedly half-mesmerized her by the gestures
that he has used to enhance the effect of his reading. The

daguerreotypist knows that "he could establish an influence over this good, pure, and simple child, as dangerous, and perhaps as disastrous, as that which the carpenter of his legend had acquired and exercised over the ill-fated Alice." But Holgrave "forbade himself to twine that one link more, which might have rendered his spell over Phoebe indissoluble."[13] In awakening Phoebe with a slight upward gesture of his hand, Holgrave chooses to lift the Pyncheon curse.

The deep sleep of 100 years is over. By the light of the rising moon in the garden, "the commonplace characteristics—which, at noontide, it seemed to have taken a century of sordid life to accumulate—were now transfigured by a charm of romance. A hundred mysterious years were whispering among the leaves. . . ." The simple, tender gesture awakens beauty. After laboring together in the garden for weeks, Holgrave and Phoebe see it for the first time: "It seems to me . . . that I never watched the coming of so beautiful an eve, and never felt anything so very much like happiness as at this moment. After all, what a good world we live in! How good, and beautiful! How young it is, too. . . ."[14]

"The Sleeping Beauty" is subtitled "Little Briar-Rose." The princess is called a briar-rose because at fifteen, she is both mischievous and tender. In *The House of the Seven Gables*, the rose comes to signify Phoebe and her beauty. The blossom also unites Phoebe with Alice: "When Phoebe was quite dressed, she peeped out of the window, and saw a rose-bush in the garden. Being a very tall one, and of luxurious growth, it had been propt up against the side of the house and was literally covered with a rare and very beautiful species of white rose . . . the whole rose-bush looked as if it had been brought from Eden, that very summer, together with the mould in which it grew. The truth was, nevertheless, that it had been planted by Alice Pyncheon—she was Phoebe's great-great-grand-aunt. . . ."[15] Clifford makes Phoebe the Little Briar-Rose when, trying to make his own slight happiness real to himself, he says to her, "Give me a rose, that I may press its thorns, and prove myself awake, by the sharp touch of pain!"[16]

Before realizing the deeper truths of "The Sleeping Beauty"—that is, before knowing Sophia Peabody—Hawthorne had apparently interpreted the legend in the light of reform movements and social issues. The hedge of thorns then signified a kind of "false consciousness" that reformers impaled themselves on. In the tale "The Procession of Life," Hawthorne observes that "each sect surrounds its own righteousness with a hedge of thorns. It is difficult for the good Christian to acknowledge the good Pagan. . . ."[17]

Hawthorne referred to many reformers and idealists as "owls" and "bats." These were the unfortunates who had cut themselves off from the richness of experience for the sake of the one true cause. By galvanizing the forces of the personality into one relentless will, these "crooked sticks" found in reforming activity an outlet for a will to dominate: "It would be endless to describe the herd of real or self-styled reformers that . . . had got possession of some crystal fragment of truth, the brightness of which so dazzled them that they could see nothing else in the wide universe. Here were men whose faith had embodied itself in the form of a potato; and others whose long beards had a deep spiritual significance. Here was the abolitionist, brandishing his one idea like an iron flail. . . ."[18]

The country was filled with people willing to attack the thorn hedge in order to force beauty to awaken. Hawthorne considered these to be spiritually dead. These were like the kings' sons of the fable, who stuck fast in the hedge of thorns and perished miserably because the time was not right. But the writer never lost his compassion: "Yet, withal, the heart of the stanchest conservative, unless he abjured his fellowship with man, could hardly have helped throbbing in sympathy with the spirit that pervaded these innumerable theorists."[19]

Judge Jaffrey Pyncheon is a model conservative who has "abjured his fellowship with man" in his "hot fellness of purpose." He and his friends ". . . are practised politicians, every man of them, and skilled to adjust those preliminary measures, which steal from the people, without its knowledge, the power of choosing its own rulers." Long familiar with politicians—"these strange malignants"—Hawthorne compares the Judge to Ixion in the Greek legend, who murdered his father-in-law in order to avoid paying the bridal gifts that he had promised.[20] Hawthorne must have despaired that, in dealing with these politicians, reformers were mere appendages—ornamental talkers and deluded men uttering democratic pieties from the cryptic and lethal depths of the American hedge of thorns.

At the Old Manse in Concord, receiving little recompense for his literary efforts, Hawthorne tended a vegetable garden—to save money on food. He spent two hours daily weeding. Weeds are very frequently mentioned in *The House of the Seven Gables*.[21] "The sordid and ugly luxuriance of gigantic weeds" is Hawthorne's modernized hedge of thorns. In the Pyncheon garden are plants "growing there in a wilderness of neglect, and obstructing one another's development [as if often the parallel case in human society] by their uneducated entanglement and confusion." Weeds represent past evil acts: "The evil of these departed years would naturally have sprung up again, in such rank weeds [symbolic of the transmitted vices of society] as are always prone to root themselves about human dwellings." The rampant hedge of thorns that so overwhelms the king's palace in "The Sleeping Beauty" is reflected in Hawthorne's description of Phoebe's chamber, "all overgrown with the desolation, which watches to obliterate every trace of man's happier hours."[22]

"The Sleeping Beauty" dramatizes the reality of fulfillment: Hawthorne insists on this possibility. There is nothing grand and glorious about this medieval legend. It does not begin with "Once upon a time" but with "A long time ago." It does not end with "And they lived happily ever after," but with "And they lived contented until the end of their days." There is no "prince charming," merely one more "king's son." He wanders by accident into the land and hears an old man talking about the thorn hedge. This king's son does not know why he is there. But he has come "in the fullness of time," and that is all that matters. We are not given his name.

Enter Holgrave, the daguerreotypist. He is not magnificent. But he does see that "there is a wonderful insight in heaven's broad and simple sunshine." And even if there was "a paragraph in a penny-paper, the other day, accusing him of making a speech, full of wild and disorganizing matter, at a meeting of his banditti-like associates," still the young man checks the growth of the wild weeds in the Pyncheon garden "by a degree of careful labor, bestowed daily and systematically." It is pleasant to see "this young man, with so much faith in himself."[23] Like the king's son, Holgrave has led the existence of a nameless, uncommitted wanderer, visiting Italy and parts of France and Germany, "continually changing his whereabouts, and, therefore responsible neither to public opinion nor to individuals—putting off one exterior, and snatching up another, to be soon shifted for a third—he had never violated the innermost man, but had carried his conscience along with him."[24] Indeed, Holgrave seems to be an avatar of "the stubborn old Puritan, Integrity," as Hepzibah thinks, perhaps capable of being "the champion of a crisis." The daguerreotypist does not reveal his identity as a Maule until the very end and claims not to know precisely why he has come to lodge in the House of the Seven Gables—even if he does speak of a drama of retribution for the wrongs of long ago and expresses a foreboding sense of catastrophe in an ominous "fifth act" to come. So Hawthorne gives an unbelieving age a vagrant adventurer as a modern knight-errant for the "Legend prolonging itself."

After years of exploring the possibilities of reform through politics, communal living, and children's literature, Hawthorne chose to put his trust in a beneficent Providence. The writer had settled on an "all good things in time" stance. Only "in the fullness of time" is it possible for the king's son to awaken beauty. In speaking of Holgrave's future prospects, Hawthorne speaks for himself as well: "He would still have faith in man's brightening destiny, and perhaps love him all the better, as he should recognize his helplessness in his own behalf; and the haughty faith, with which he began life, would be well bartered for a far humbler one, at its close, in discerning that man's best-directed effort accomplishes a kind of dream, while God is the sole worker of realities."[25]

Family life considerably tempered Hawthorne, allowing him to come to full maturity as an artist. While writing *The House of the Seven Gables* in the autumn of 1850, with Sophia pregnant with Rose, Hawthorne must have remembered the early miscarriage before the birth of Una, his first child. The difficulty may have been caused by falls Sophia took while ice-skating on the Concord River, but for some time, both despaired of bearing living children.[26] The opening line of the legend of the Sleeping Beauty must have had enormous significance: "A long time ago there were a king and queen who said every day, Ah, if only we had a child! but they never had one." While Nathaniel was playing with his children one afternoon at this time, son Julian became known as "little Prince Rose-red." And the yet unborn Rose Hawthorne, with the "thorn" in her last name, obviously bears the inspiration of "Little Briar-Rose."[27]

Sophia Amelia Peabody was Nathaniel Hawthorne's living sleeping beauty. They first met as children of the neighborhood, playing in Salem's Charter Street burying ground. Hawthorne describes this time in the opening scenes of his late romance *Doctor Grimshawe's Secret*. They tumbled wildly over the tombs, picking dandelions and chasing butterflies, playing hide-and-seek amongst the slate and the marble. They memorized verses on the headstones and spelled out the names on them. Sophia shared Nathaniel's increasingly common reveries, sitting quietly, holding her Persian kitten. The cemetery held the graves of Nathaniel's ancestors, including that of the Salem witch-trial judge Col. John Hathorne. Some time later, Hawthorne read "An aged man of nineteen years" on the gravestone of Nathaniel Mather. "It affected me deeply, when I had cleared away the grass from the half-buried stone, and read the name" of this "hard student." The burying ground was surrounded by a high wooden fence, and a little gate lead to Sophia's house, through a neglected but fertile garden, to the back door. She lived in a square-fronted, three-storied frame house with massive chimneys and small-paned windows. Nathaniel must have cherished deep memories of this ground, for he proposed to Sophia on its granite entrance steps.

As a young woman, Sophia was small and graceful, impulsive, quick, intuitive, delighting in companionship. Rougish, often smiling and half-laughing, she had a friendly wit, though her blue-grey eyes were sometimes observed to turn a distinctly darker shade with silent opposition. She brushed her chestnut-brown hair every morning for an hour in what she called her studio, on the third floor of the sunny side of the house, overlooking the burying ground. Here she painted, read, and often slept in a hammock stretched in the corner. Sophia was confined to her room every afternoon almost all year with the blinding headaches and the "cannonading of her temples." She was an invalid. Not entirely helpless, she was forever sending people little gifts, flowers and notes, and receiving visitors among her pictures and flowers:

> Sometimes her whole day passed in a kind of unreal pageant of affection. She awakened in the morning pleased with the elm tree that grew outside her window, and the robin that sang in its branches, the clematis that climbed in her window, and the flowers that people brought her. Ellen Barstow, Hawthorne's cousin Nancy's child, brought her a crimson rose. Her sister Mary brought her a handful of flowers in the morning and she crowed over them awhile before she arose. Mary Channing brought her a Scotch rose. Sally Gardiner brought her an armload of roses. She listened to George Hillard talk agreeable nonsense—he said the postmaster of Cambridge was an old man, a hundred and forty years old, who reminded him of nothing sharpened to a point.[28]

To kill her pain, Sophia was laced first with the tinctures of opium, paregoric, and laudanum, in the allopathic or heroic system of large doses, then with mercury and arsenic, and finally with hyoscyamus, or henbane: "Ever since her early childhood, when Sophia had been given a good deal of paregoric to ease difficult teething, her father had feared that he had given her too much sedative. He gave her sedatives now, at the insistence of her mother, but with increasing reluctance because he had become interested in homeopathy with its theory that 'like cures like' and its use of drugs in small doses only. Dr. Peabody was pleased with the 'best European leeches' and so was Sophia."[29]

Sophia's sister Elizabeth said that the doctors in Boston "one after another, tried their hands at curing her, and she went through courses of their poisons, each one bringing her to death's door, and leaving her less able to cope with the pain. But the endurance of her physical constitution defied all the poisons of the *materia medica,*—mercury, arsenic, opium, hyoscyamus, and all. Her last allopathic physician was Dr. Walter Channing, who limited himself to fighting the pain without attempting a radical cure."

The hyoscyamus—a drug used to extract confessions from criminals—produced a twilight sleep. *Hyoscyamus niger,* or black henbane, contains the alkaloids hyoscyamine, hyoscine, with atropine throughout. This plant was a staple in medieval poison potions and witches' brews, causing watering of the mouth, rapid pulse, headache, nausea, and fits of madness with delirium, convulsions, coma, and death. Elizabeth says that "in 1830, when she [Sophia] was living on hyoscyamus, which did her less harm than any other drug, she was able to come downstairs occasionally and into the schoolroom on drawing-days. . . ." This drug affected Sophia's feverish reactions to nature: the abnormally bright colors, the lurid moonlight, the vividly clear songs of birds. Here Sophia describes a sunrise:

When I first opened my eyes, I found the eastern and northern horizon blushing deeply at the coming glory. Just above the soft orange and celestial green lay a long, heavy cloud, which I knew would become illuminated

very soon. I had a short nap between, and dreamed of
watching a sunrise, and that the sky was covered with
clouds shaped like coffins! When I awoke, I could not
help shouting. That dun mass was a magnificent pile of
wrought gold and amethyst, fretted, quivering, gor-
geous. The east looked like a wreck of precious stones,
only the dyes were not of the earth. Below, deep orange
and that tender green melted into one another; just
above, rolled out this dazzling fold of unimaginable glory,
and, higher still, floated soft fleecy clouds in the pale,
infinite azure. Not the slightest shroud of mist lay upon
anything. As soon as the Sun's crowned head rose up
(and I watched it rise), it seemed as if myriads of dia-
monds were at that moment flung upon the earth, for
the dew-drops each reflected the smile of the mighty
Alchemist. Truly he turns everything into gold![30]

Mrs. Peabody, Sophia's mother, came from a line of
prominent industrialists, mostly in glassmaking, who had lost
their fortunes after the Revolution. She was a confirmed Uni-
tarian, thus losing even more financial and social standing in
this family of Calvinists. Mrs. Peabody had towering social
ambitions and pretensions, and she made Sophia a part of her
plan to recover high standing in society. Maintaining an invalid in the family was a mark of status in the nineteenth-
century upper classes; accordingly, Mrs. Peabody felt inclined
to force Sophia into this role. She sought to keep her daughter
an eternal invalid by continually exaggerating the dangers of
independence, always trying to cripple her will. Robert Cantwell says that Mrs. Peabody was "a strong-minded woman
who impressed upon her children her iron characterizations
of their abilities, like clothes which did not quite fit them."
Sophia was set out as the family sacrifice:

The favorite pastime of my aunts Emily and Matilda was
to torment me; and whenever they could take me captive, I was led off for cruel sport. The mischievous gleam

of their dark eyes, and the wonderful rivulets of dark curls flowing over their crimson cheeks, are painted on my inner tablets in fixed colors. Sometimes they opened a great book (which I now fear was the Bible) and commanded me to read a lesson. If I miscalled the letters in trying to spell the words, they shouted in derision. My sensitiveness doubtless incited them to ingenious devices to mortify and frighten me. One day they asked me if I would like to see the most beautiful of gardens, blooming with the sweetest, gayest flowers; and when I gratefully and joyfully assented, trusting them without misgiving, they opened a door and gave me a sudden push, which sent me falling down several steps into utter darkness. Another time they took me into a courtyard full of turkeys, and drove the creatures, gobbling like so many fiends, towards me. I expected to be devoured at once, and my distress was immeasurable; and the enjoyment of the young ladies was complete. Their mocking laughter made me feel ashamed of being miserable.[31]

Young and essentially healthy, Sophia resisted the attack by her kinswomen and mother with constant and painful headaches—she was already a semi-invalid at the age of nine. The exploiting and self-complacent Mrs. Peabody carefully lectured that suffering is woman's lot, that it is the will of God after the Fall of Adam, that it was Sophia's duty to be "resigned" and not to be so "wickedly resisting God's will." The hypocritical Mrs. Peabody explained, apparently reasonably, that the pain she inflicted was successfully ". . . correcting, subduing, eradicating self-sufficiency. . . .And now that your Father and mine sees fit to give you the enjoyment of tolerable health, you will devote all the energies of your enthusiastic and glowing mind to His Service and Glory."[32] This smug announcement was met with torrents of tears, what the shamed Sophia called her "Thunder-gusts."

It was to little avail; Sophia was hedged in everywhere by stern warnings that amounted to threats; she must not laugh, must not waltz because the shock might do serious injury if repeated, must avoid the night air and the bracing fresh air by day. Sophia was denied an active part of the work in moving to the Charter Street house, ordered to "sit in her sweet room at her center table and look straight into Colonel Pickman's garden of flowers." To the violent headaches, nausea, and drugs was added an almost nutrition-free diet of white bread and rice. This continual domineering took its inevitable toll. Sophia became "resigned" to an early death and convinced herself that she would never be a burden to any man. Mrs. Peabody had all but convinced Sophia that all men were domineering, inconsiderate, and hurting and that in the power struggle of the sexes, the only alternative open to women besides humiliating submission was a manipulative ill health. Small wonder, then, that Sophia agreed to let her engagement to Nathaniel Hawthorne continue only on the condition that the marriage would be contingent upon her complete recovery from a twenty-year illness: "If God intends us to marry, He will let me be cured; if not, it will be a sign that it is not best."

The spirited Sophia resorted to travel for her health and happiness. The favored tactic was to claim to be "just visiting" any given family, in order to avoid the mother's "tearful protest," and to then develop excuses to extend her escape. After two months of pleading in 1825, and only with her father's final insistence, Sophia traveled over a hundred miles by chaise to New Hampshire over wild roads and never felt better. Another trip in 1827 took Sophia to her aunt Mary Palmer Tyler, living on Putney Street near the Common in Brattleboro, Vermont. Sophia's many young cousins went mountain climbing and horseback riding with her until Mrs. Peabody wrote: "The high state of excitement you are in is not exactly the thing for your head. . . . Come home now, and live awhile upon the past."[33] Sophia was eighteen years old. Three years later, Sophia moved to a studio in Dedham and successfully supported herself by painting. She enjoyed a "fervent happiness" in her creativity, but returned to Salem again when Mrs. Peabody could no longer bear her daughter's happiness.

The invalid would not be allowed to teach drawing in her sisters' school near Boston.

Finally despairing of her life, sister Elizabeth arranged for Sophia to sail to Cuba in December 1833 for an extended visit to friends who owned a hacienda outside Havana. Mrs. Peabody told the adventurer on departure that she could not be expected to survive the voyage, even without shipwreck, and that she would die in a strange land. Sophia soon rode forty-five miles on horseback in one day, racing to the hacienda and feeling only slightly tired and sore the next day. But upon returning, completely healthy, the next year, Sophia would write to her sister Elizabeth: "I had an indefinite hope that such a great stir as a voyage to Cuba would alter the state of things but they are settling down again."[34]

While courting Sophia, Nathaniel wrote her: "Where art thou? My heart searches for thee. . . . It seems as if all evil things had more power over thee when I am away."[35] In later years, an acquaintance of Hawthorne would say that the writer had a cat's ability to see in the dark—as certain it was that he needed that faculty in order to avoid all the snares of the Peabody clan. "When Hawthorne married Sophia he rescued her from harder captors than the wicked ogre of the fairy tales—drugs, headaches, years in bed, and more dangerous than any, the nervous, brittle, affected aestheticism of the New England intellectuals of the time."[36] His sleeping beauty! Hawthorne accomplished this by love and by long walks to parties in winter on Chestnut Street in Salem, by fresh, open air and common consideration. Sophia the slight and pale took on substance, better color, and confidence, and the pain fell away.

After Nathaniel's enormous efforts to secure the necessary financial footing, their wedding day was set.

> . . . They were to be married on the twenty-seventh of June, the month of roses and perfect bloom, as Sophia wrote to Margaret Fuller in announcing the event.

Then, on the very day originally appointed for the wedding, Hawthorne received a note from Sophia saying that she was ill. There was delay after delay, Hawthorne eager to know when the minister was to appear for the ceremony, and yet assuring Sophia that he would patiently bear the postponement, and counseling her to keep her heart quiet—not to excite herself in this removal of her household gods. A thousand ages hence they would be only in the honeymoon of their marriage. Nevertheless, he was himself restless, and he had a night haunted by ghastly dreams in which he dreamed that Sophia had been hypnotized, and so agitated was he that he awoke in an absolute quake.[37]

Perhaps Hawthorne had heard that Dr. Peabody's partner in dentistry, one Fiske, had attempted to induce a deep hypnotic sleep in the gentle and compliant Sophia, only to be surprised and disappointed by her ability to resist.

Nightmares aside, the waking reality was even worse. Mrs. Peabody had informed her daughter on her prospective wedding day that she must never have a child because if she did, it would kill her and that she would never paint again if she married because she would be too tired. The badgering was so intense, Sophia took to her bed. Mrs. Peabody hoped that the wedding would be delayed indefinitely, but Sophia merely called for the family doctor and set July 9, 1842, for her nuptial appointment. The "prisoner to pain" had slipped away.

The enchantment that Nathaniel Hawthorne escaped was his own talent, his penchant for exploring social quandries—the "moral picturesque" as he called it. The search for artistic and spiritual enlightenment often seemed hollow and false, even antagonistic to the traditional social values: "the settled, sober, careful gladness of a man by his own fireside, with those around him whose welfare is committed to his trust. . . ." The young Hawthorne never forgot that "the truly wise, after all their speculations, will be led into the common path, and, in homage to the human nature that pervades them, will gather gold, and till the earth, and set out trees, and build a house."[38]

Hawthorne presents this terrible conflict in Clifford Pyncheon. Clifford is the character who simply lacks the moral strength to prevent his love of the beautiful, the elegant, and the purely aesthetic from blighting his own simple human sympathies. He lacks "the heart, the will, and conscience, to fight a battle with the world" for his soul. Clifford worships beauty, but abandons human obligations because they are not always pretty. He cannot bear to look at his unfashionably attired and nearsightedly scowling but deserving and devoted sister. Hawthorne proposes that there was poetic justice, if not strictly legal justice, in Clifford's thirty years' imprisonment: "It is even possible—for similar cases have often happened—that if Clifford, in his foregoing life, had enjoyed the means of cultivating his taste to its utmost perfectibility, that subtle attribute might, before this period, have completely eaten out or filed away his affections. Shall we venture to pronounce, therefore, that his long and black calamity may not have had a redeeming drop of mercy, at the bottom?"[39]

Clifford's possibility troubled Hawthorne, but the absolute lack or sleep of beauty terrified him. He never turned a blind eye to the brutal things done by men who had capitulated to the dominant American ethic of convenience, gold, and despair. The cold and simple, commonsense, practical, grasping, and materialistic understanding of many citizens was something to be resented and outwitted. In "The Artist of the Beautiful," Owen Warland sees the perfection of his craft, an exquisite mechanical toy butterfly, crushed by a baby. It is Hawthorne's most dramatic depiction of the pure, destroying hand of infantile materialism. The American compulsion to destroy what is beautiful is founded on that Puritan terror of beauty as a possible trap set by Satan. Hawthorne knew our culture of fear and outwitted it.

Struggling to overcome his own puritanical fear of happiness, Nathaniel Hawthorne discovered for the first time, with Sophia, that beauty is not a delusion. In the spring in Concord, he looked on the swallows chattering in the dim, sun-streaked interior of a lofty barn. He planted his trees: larkins, elms and oak, pitch pines and firs and white birch: "Indeed we are but shadows; we are not endowed with real life, and all that seems most real about us is but the thinnest substance of a dream—till the heart be touched. That touch creates us—then we begin to be—thereby we are beings of reality and inheritors of eternity."[40]

But *The House of the Seven Gables* is not simply an extended meditation on the dangers and purposes of beauty as revealed in the depths of the old tale so honorably recorded by the brothers Grimm. The artist remembered the beloved, corrupt Salem. The town's name means "Peace," but after his ritual-like sacking at the Custom House, and the furious response of the local newspapers, politicians and clergy to *The Scarlet Letter*, Hawthorne thought otherwise. After the Salem people "at two several attacks" had permitted him "to be deliberately lied down," he wished to "bid farewell forever to this abominable city": "I detest this town so much that I hate to go into the streets, or to have the people see me. . . . I feel an infinite contempt for them, and probably have expressed more of it than I intended; for my preliminary chapter has caused the greatest uproar that ever happened here since witch-times." He half-expected the crowds to tar and feather him: "from such judges as my fellow-citizens, I should look upon it as a higher honor than a laurel-crown."[41]

On May 23, 1850, the Hawthorne family took the train from the castle station in Salem to Lenox in the Berkshire Hills of western Massachusetts. The writer called this retreat "Moving their household gods from Salem," an allusion to Virgil's *Aeneid*, in which the Roman hero Aeneas follows an ancient custom, moving his household gods from the sacked and burning Troy, bearing his father, Anchises, on his back.[42] In *The House of the Seven Gables*, the legend of the Golden Bough from the *Aeneid* appears with the morning sun: ". . . a reflected gleam, struggling through the boughs of the elm-tree."[43] There is another allusion to the epic poem in the first impression given by Jaffrey Pyncheon: ". . . you could feel just as certain that he was opulent . . . as if you had seen him touching the twigs of the Pyncheon-elm, and, Midas-like, transmuting them to gold."[44] This ancestral elm survives the five-day northeaster intact,

> . . . except a single branch, that, by the earlier change with which the elm-tree sometimes prophesies the autumn, had been transmuted to bright gold. It was like the golden branch that gained Aeneas and the Sibyl admittance into Hades.
>
> This one mystic branch hung down before the main-entrance of the seven gables, so nigh the ground, that any passer-by might have stood on tiptoe and plucked it off. Presented at the door, it would have been a symbol of his right to enter and be made acquainted with all the secrets of the house.[45]

In Virgil's *Aeneid*, Aeneas descends into the Lower World and sees that "an elm-tree loomed there, shadowy and huge,/ The aged boughs outspread, beneath whose leaves,/ Men say, the false dreams cling, thousands on thousands."[46]

Hawthorne not only links his Pyncheon elm to the Virgil elm; he also recollects that in "The Sleeping Beauty," the curse settles on the whole world: "And the wind fell, and on the trees before the castle, not a leaf moved again." But the Pyncheon elm will survive the terrible storm, and beauty will return: "The Pyncheon-elm, throughout its great circumference, was all alive, and full of the morning sun and a sweetly tempered little breeze, which lingered within this verdant sphere, and set a thousand leafy tongues a-whispering all at once." The elm "whispered unintelligible prophecies."[47]

Themes from the *Aeneid*, interpreted in Nathaniel Hawthorne's mythopoetic mind, abound in *The House of the Seven Gables*. Clifford becomes a second Aeneas: "this poor, forlorn voyager from the Islands of the Blest, in a frail bark, on a tempestuous sea, had been flung, by the last mountain-wave of his shipwreck, into a quiet harbor. There, as he lay more than half-lifeless on the strand, the fragrance of an earthly rosebud had come to his nostrils, and, as odors will, had summoned up reminiscences or visions of all the living and breathing beauty, amid which he should have had his home."[48]

Translating the *Aeneid* for entrance to Bowdoin College in 1820, at the age of sixteen, was a deep revelation and consolation for Nathaniel, the forlorn son of lost seafarers. He was ever haunted by the feeling that his father had never been properly buried at home, in Salem. The elder Nathaniel Hathorne, a ship captain, had died of yellow fever in Surinam just before sailing for home in 1808, when his son was four years old. The first six books of Virgil's epic poem speak of Aeneas's moral quest, the almost fatal sea journey, and his death-celebrating funeral rites. The famous image of Aeneas bearing his father on his shoulders from the burning Troy and the poem's overwhelming stress on funeral rites are echoed in Holgrave's talk of the past: "It lies upon the Present like a giant's dead body! In fact, the case is just as if a young giant were compelled to waste all his strength in carrying about the corpse of the old giant, his grandfather, who died a long while ago, and only needs to be decently buried. Just think, a moment; and it will startle you to see what slaves we are to bygone times—to Death, if we give the matter the right word!"[49]

The elder Nathaniel Hathorne's death marked his son for life: "The world is cold," said the writer, "and I am an almshouse child."

> If you know anything of me, you know how I sprang out of mystery, akin to none, a thing concocted out of the elements, without visible agency—how, all through my boyhood, I was alone; how I grew up without a root, yet continually longing for one—longing to be connected with somebody—and never feeling myself so. . . . I have tried to keep down this yearning, to stifle it, annihilate it, with making a position for myself, with being my own

past; but I cannot overcome this natural horror of being a creature floating in the air, attached to nothing; ever this feeling that there is no reality in the life and fortunes, good or bad, of a being so unconnected. There is not even a grave, not a heap of dry bones, not a pinch of dust, with which I can claim connection.[50]

Hawthorne feared that he should "leave no son to inherit my share in life, with a better sense of its privileges and duties, when his father should vanish like a bubble."[51]

Hawthorne inherited his father's sea journals—a source of inspiration and a spur to the writer's literary impulse. The elder Nathaniel addressed couplets and quatrains to his young wife back in Salem in these journals. With the *Perseverence* docked in Manila, he wrote: "Lowering Clouds appear/ And angry Jove deforms the inclement Year." While translating the *Aeneid*, the son thought of going to sea himself and played at writing a ship's log. He copied his father's ornate script in one journal, practicing. In the hand-printed *Spectator*— a newsletter of his own devising—in 1820, in answer to the question "What then is Benevolence?" he gives "It is to protect the fatherless, and to make the Widow's heart to sing for joy.'" In an essay entitled, "Autumnal," he asks, "Must we slumber to awake no more?"[52]

Many of Hawthorne's tales deal with the sudden departure, by a character, from the ordinary way. The question is often whether or not there will be a successful return to the true inner self. In these inventions, we see the child who, in the years following his father's death, made up stories for his sisters and ended them with "And then I'll go away and never come back." His literary obsequies began with these and with the quatrain he buried a cat with. There is an early concern for proper burial in his ritualistic repetition of a favorite line from *Richard III:* "Stand back, my lord, and let the coffin pass!" The spiritual quests in his childhood favorites, John Bunyan's *Pilgrim's Progress* and Edmund Spenser's *Faerie Queene*, became associated with his father's last journey. This child again dominates the author of *The House of the Seven Gables* passage in which Hepzibah, in flight from her house, has "the wretched consciousness of being adrift," while "wandering all abroad, on precisely such a pilgrimage as a child often meditates, to the world's end."[53] Surinam may well have been the world's end.

The circumstances of Captain Hathorne's death are presented here: "Hardly a week after his decease, one of the Cunard steamers brought intelligence of the death, by cholera, of Judge Pyncheon's son, just at the point of embarkation for his native land." Hepzibah also has "an uncle—who had sailed for India, fifty years before, and never been heard of since. . . ." Both Hawthorne's uncles—John Manning and Daniel Hathorne, maternal and paternal—had been lost at sea. Finally, only one month elapsed from Margaret Fuller's drowning on July 19, 1850, and Hawthorne's measured sentence "In this republican country, amid the fluctuating waves of our social life, somebody is always at the drowning-point."[54]

The central image in the *Aeneid* is the serpent.[55] Hawthorne's serpent references strike a Virgilian aspect. Holgrave mentions "the drama which, for almost two hundred years, has been dragging its slow length over the ground, where you and I now tread"—the drama of the Pyncheon-Maule vengeance. Jaffrey Pyncheon's "sultry, dog-day heat" of benevolence radiates from his heart, making him "very much like a serpent, which, as a preliminary to fascination, is said to fill the air with his peculiar odor." The scissor-grinder's wheel "issued an intense and spiteful prolongation of a hiss, as fierce as those emitted by Satan and his compeers in Pandemonium. . . . It was an ugly, little, venemous serpent of a noise. . . ."[56]

In the chapter "The Arched Window," the political procession that "trailed its length of trampling footsteps" past the House of the Seven Gables is a kind of serpent. It "might so fascinate" Clifford as to induce him to hurl himself to his death from the arched window in a misguided effort to join the throng below. Hawthorne's memories of politics in Salem were still painful, so he describes the procession as "trampling." He once told Horace Conolly, whom he regarded as his most subtle betrayer in Salem, "I don't reckon you among my enemies, nor ever have. You are a kind of pet serpent, and must be allowed to bite now and then, that being the nature of the critter."[57] Pondering the timeless themes of the *Aeneid* in the Berkshire Hills, Hawthorne, still resenting being cast out of Salem, looked about for his personal Trojan Horse. He was not long in finding one.

On August 5, 1850, Nathaniel Hawthorne met Herman Melville: the impact shook every timber in *The House of the Seven Gables*. The presence of this brooding mariner, a poetic soul such as Hawthorne's father had been stirred the deepest memories—and doubts—of the older and happier writer. Melville's talk of the sea, of time, eternity, death, myth, and literature, his metaphysical leaping, struck Hawthorne's own particular woe. The two writers decided that the situation required not telling the truth directly. Hawthorne eventually recoiled from Melville's truth—but not before giving to *Moby Dick; or The Whale* the bitter duplicity of his literary technique for *The House of the Seven Gables*.

Writing a romance based on "The Sleeping Beauty" called for a happy ending. Two or three weeks after the publication of *The House of the Seven Gables*, Hawthorne wrote: ". . . in writing it, I suppose I was illuminated by my purpose to bring it to a prosperous close, while the gloom of the past threw its shadow along the reader's pathway."[58] This is consistent with Hawthorne's faith—despite Salem—in "man's brightening destiny." But clearly, a happy ending could never be written by the man who had said: "Be true! Be true! Be true! Show freely to the world, if not your worst, yet some trait whereby the worst may be inferred!"[59] In order to resolve this literary dilemma, Hawthorne resorted to Melville's technique of multiple levels of meaning. On November 29, 1850, he wrote that "it darkens damnably towards the close, but I shall try hard to pour some setting sunshine over it."[60]

In only ten days, toward the close of January 1851, he refashioned the better part of six chapters. He did not invent an entirely new story. Large fragments of the originally intended dark ending were placed skillfully in different contexts, making the surface story sunny enough, but without destroying the deeper meaning for careful readers, such as Herman Melville. *The House of the Seven Gables* is very close in spirit to that other allegory of the triumph of evil, *The Scarlet Letter*. It is precisely what Sophia called it in her journal: "the inevitable Fate—'the innocent suffering for the guilty' seemingly so dark yet so clear a law."[61] In order to discover Hawthorne's original depiction of this dark fate, one finds the scattered fragments of narrative and phrase and reassembles them. Only then is it seen that the innocents who suffer for the guilty are Clifford and Hepzibah.[62]

In the chapter "The Flight of Two Owls," Clifford flees from the House of the Seven Gables with Hepzibah after Judge Pyncheon's death. In Hawthorne's original draft, however, Clifford overhears the Judge tell Hepzibah that it was he who had freed him from prison, for the sole purpose of extorting from him the secret of his uncle's wealth. If Clifford will not tell, the Judge will send him to the asylum. Unable to recall the secret spring behind Colonel Pyncheon's portrait, which he had discovered as a child and the hiding place of the parchment deed to vast tracts of land, and terrified at the prospect of the asylum, Clifford flees—alone.

In the familiar story, Hepzibah leaves the judge sitting in the parlor and goes to get Clifford, but does not find him in his room. Surprised and despairing, she fantasizes the terrible thing that actually befalls Clifford in the original story: ". . . aware of the presence of his Evil Destiny, he had crept silently down the staircase, while the Judge and Hepzibah stood talking in the shop, and had softly undone the fastenings of the outer door, and made his escape into the street. . . ."[63] He goes "wandering through the city, attracting all eyes, and everybody's wonder and repugnance . . . ," incurring "the ridicule of the younger crowd." Clifford is "goaded by their taunts, their loud, shrill cries, and cruel laughter—insulted by the filth of the public ways, which they would fling upon him. . . ." The town is "almost completely water-girdled," so he discovers "the wharves stretched out towards the centre of the harbor, each wharf a solitude." He bends "one moment, over the deep, black tide" and thinks "that here was the sure refuge within his reach, and that, with a single step, or the slightest overbalance of his body, he might be forever beyond his kinsman's gripe. . . ."

In Hawthorne's original story, there was a long description of Clifford at this critical moment before leaping into the harbor. Fragments of this story survive in the final chapter, "The Arched Window," in which Clifford feels an impulse to leap from the balcony to join the political procession. He is "an impressible person, standing alone over the brink of . . . a mighty river . . . massive in its tide, and black with mystery, and, out of its depths, calling to the kindred depth within him. . . ."[64] "It might so fascinate him, that he would hardly be restrained from plunging into the surging stream. . . ." "So it proved with Clifford. He shuddered; he grew pale, he threw an appealing look. . . . At last, with tremulous limbs, he started up, set his foot . . . and, in an instant more, would have been in the . . ." Clifford is "a wild, haggard figure, his gray locks floating in the wind . . . a lonely being, estranged from his race, but now feeling himself man again, by virtue of the irrepressible instinct that possessed him. . . . But whether impelled by the species of terror, that sometimes urges its victim over the very precipice which he shrinks from, or by a natural magnetism, tending towards the great centre . . . it were not easy to decide. Both impulses might have wrought on him at once."

In the effort to pour sunshine over this damnably darkening scene, Hawthorne changed the temptation at the harbor to the attempt to leap from the arched window, which is not successful:

> But his companions, affrighted by his gesture—which was that of a man hurried away, in spite of himself—seized

Clifford's garment and held him back. Hepzibah shrieked. Phoebe, to whom all extravagance was a horror, burst into sobs and tears.

"Clifford, Clifford, are you crazy?" cried his sister.

"I hardly know, Hepzibah!" said Clifford, drawing a long breath. "Fear nothing—it is over now—but had I taken that plunge, and survived it, methinks it would have made me another man!"

Possibly, in some sense, Clifford may have been right. He needed a shock; or perhaps he required to take a deep, deep plunge into the ocean of human life, and to sink down and be covered by its profoundness, and then to emerge, sobered, invigorated, restored to the world and to himself. Perhaps, again, he required nothing less than the great final remedy—death![65]

In the original story, Clifford drowns himself and Hawthorne points to his death with irony: Judge Jaffrey Pyncheon has been suddenly given blood to drink, and the cousin's suicide is totally unavailing. Hawthorne describes the process of drowning in detail, a matter of "whirling sticks, straws, and all such trifles, round and round, right over the black depth where a dead corpse lay unseen. . . . At his decease, there is only vacancy, and a momentary eddy—very small, as compared with the apparent magnitude of the ingurgitated object—and a bubble or two, ascending out of the black depth, and bursting at the surface."[66] Hawthorne displayed such deliberate skill in pouring sunshine over these fragments to conceal his true meaning that an admiring Herman Melville could not resist modeling the sinking of the *Pequod* on the sinking of Clifford. Melville's Ishmael is slowly drawn to the vortex of the whirlpool created by the plunging ship; "Round and round, then, and ever contracting towards the buttonlike black bubble at the axis of that slowly wheeling circle, like another Ixion I did revolve. Till, gaining that vital centre, the black bubble upward burst. . . ."[67]

In describing Judge Pyncheon's sterling character and reputation as a "magnificent palace," Hawthorne observes that there, "beneath the marble pavement, in a stagnant water-puddle . . . may lie a corpse, half-decayed, and still decaying, and diffusing its death-scent all through the palace!"[68] This is the passage Hawthorne has in mind when, years later in England, observing the deformed and diseased children in an almshouse, he confronted the deepest threat to his faith:

> It might almost make a man doubt the existence of his own soul, to observe how Nature has flung these little wretches into the street and left them there, so evidently regarding them as nothing worth, and how all mankind acquiesce in the great mother's estimate of her offspring. For, if they are to have no immortality, what superior claim can I assert for mine? And how difficult to believe that anything so precious as a germ of immortal growth can have been buried under this dirt-heap, plunged into this cesspool of misery and vice! Without an infinite faith, there seemed as much prospect of a blessed futurity for those hideous bugs and many-footed worms [which one finds under rotting plants] as for these brethren of our humanity and co-heirs of all our heavenly inheritance. Ah, what a mystery! Slowly, slowly, as after groping at the bottom of a deep, noisome, stagnant pool, my hope struggles upward to the surface, bearing the half-drowned body of a child along with it, and heaving it aloft for its life, and my own life, and all our lives. Unless these slime-clogged nostrils can be made capable of inhaling celestial air, I know not how the purest and most intellectual of us can reasonably expect ever to taste a breath of it. The whole question of eternity is staked there. If a single one of those helpless little ones be lost, the world is lost![69]

In a dirty Liverpool almshouse, a ragged little girl walked up to the elderly, courtly American consul, Nathaniel Hawthorne, and held out her arms to be picked up. "The world is cold," wrote the author years later, "and I am an almshouse child."

In Clifford Pyncheon, Hawthorne confronts his deepest fears; with Hepzibah, he creates the finest American tragedy. She will be executed for witchcraft. Hawthorne very carefully builds up a demonic aura about Hepzibah: ". . . she expected to minister to the wants of the community, unseen, like a disembodied divinity, or enchantress, holding forth her bargains to the reverential and awe-stricken purchaser, in an invisible hand. . . . She now issued forth, as would appear, to defend the entrance, looking, we must needs say, amazingly like the dragon which, in fairy tales, is wont to be the guardian over an enchanted beauty."[70] Uncle Venner is described as "a kind of familiar of the house." The word *familiar* signifies the companion of a witch—usually a black cat or, in medieval lore, a goat.

Hepzibah's master, that old Deluder, Satan, calls her: "She was suddenly startled by the tinkling alarum—high, sharp, and irregular—of a little bell. The maiden lady arose upon her feet, as pale as a ghost at cock-crow; for she was an enslaved spirit, and this the talisman to which she owed obedience." This "ugly and spiteful little din" betrays the advent of the Prince of Darkness:

> But, at this instant, the shop-bell, right over her head, tinkled as if it were bewitched. The old gentlewoman's heart seemed to be attached to the same steel-spring; for it went through a series of sharp jerks, in unison with the sound. The door was thrust open, although no human form was perceptible on the other side of the half-window. Hepzibah, nevertheless, stood at a gaze, with her hands clasped, looking very much as if she had summoned up an evil spirit and were afraid, yet resolved, to hazard the encounter.
>
> "Heaven help me!" she groaned mentally. "Now is my hour of need!"[71]

Satan has come to tempt his servant with the riches of the world, in an American version of the temptation of Christ during his forty days in the Wilderness: "Some malevolent

spirit, doing his utmost to drive Hepzibah mad, unrolled before her imagination a kind of panorama, representing the
great thoroughfare of a city, all astir with customers. So many
and so magnificent shops as there were!"[72] The Pyncheon cent
shop is very poor.

Hepzibah has "a sense of inevitable doom" about her
nearsighted frown, or scowl, for good reason. This "scowl—a
strange contortion of the brow—which, by people who did
not know her, would probably have been interpreted as an
expression of bitter anger and ill-will" has "done Miss Hepzibah a very ill-office, in establishing her character as an ill-
tempered old maid . . . The custom of the shop fell off,
because a story got abroad that she soured her small beer and
other damageable commodities, by scowling on them." Moreover, in "her great life-trial . . . the testimony in regard to
her scowl was frightfully important."

The laboring man Dixey testifies against her in his rough
voice, "Why, her face—I've seen it; for I dug her garden for
her, one year—her face is enough to frighten Old Nick himself, if he had ever so great a mind to trade with her. People
can't stand it, I tell you! She scowls dreadfully, reason or
none, out of pure ugliness of temper!" One Mrs. Gubbins also
condemns Hepzibah. Hawthorne describes this demonic
neighbor: "there came a fat woman. . . . Her face glowed with
fire-heat; and, it being a pretty warm morning, she bubbled
and hissed, as it were, as if all a-fry with chimney-warmth,
and summer-warmth, and the warmth of her own corpulent
velocity." She angrily jarred and outraged the shop bell, mut-
tered, "The deuce take Old Maid Pyncheon!" and "took her
departure, still brimming over with hot wrath. . . ."[73]

Judge Pyncheon tells Hepzibah that he has arranged to
have Clifford's "deportment and habits constantly and carefully overlooked"—in order to persecute him more effectively.
"The butcher, the baker, the fishmonger, some of the customers of your shop, and many a prying old woman, have told
me several of the secrets of your interior." When both Clifford
and the Judge die, these eyewitnesses will turn their accu-

sations on Hepzibah. She is accused specifically of the murder of Jaffrey Pyncheon, since the Judge died in her parlor. The "good lady on the opposite side of the street" will be there at the trial to explain that ". . . there's been a quarrel between him and Hepzibah, this many a day, because he won't give her a living. That's the main reason of her setting up a cent-shop." Dixey will be there to implicate Clifford in the murder as well: "A certain cousin of his may have been at his old tricks. And Old Maid Pyncheon having got herself in debt by the cent-shop—and the Judge's pocket-book being well-filled—and bad blood amongst them already! Put all these things together, and see what they make!"[74]

As one of the Judge's spies, the butcher assaults the House of the Seven Gables, prying about "every accessible door" and the window in his attempts to get a glimpse of Clifford. He sees the Judge himself sitting in the parlor—dead—and thinks that it is Clifford, whom he curses as "Old Maid Pyncheon's bloody brother." Hawthorne's literary duplicity here convinces the careless reader that the butcher's assault is motivated by a desire to please Hepzibah with "his sweetbread of lamb." The truth is, Clifford is the lamb sacrificed to the butcher's greed.[75]

"The Flight of Two Owls" is filled with allusions to death and mortality. It records Hepzibah's sensations on her way to the place of execution and to that "gimlet-eyed" gentleman who will take her life. This acerbic old conservative thinks that the newly invented telegraph is a great thing, "particularly as regards the detection of bank-robbers and murderers . . . " Hawthorne gives him the gimlet eye, which traditionally could bore into a person to cause paralysis or death. There was " . . . a moral sensation, mingling itself with the physical chill, and causing her to shake more in spirit than in body," and " . . . the wretched consciousness of being adrift. She had lost the faculty of self-guidance . . . " As they went on, the feeling of indistinctness and unreality kept dimly hovering roundabout her, and so diffusing itself into her system that one of her hands was hardly palpable to the touch of the other. . . ." She whispered to herself, again and again—"Am I awake?—Am I awake?" And ". . . the bell rang out its hasty peal, so well expressing the brief summons which life vouchsafes to us, in its hurried career. . . . At a little distance stood a wooden church, black with age, and in a dismal state of ruin and decay, with broken windows, a great rift through the main-body of the edifice, and a rafter dangling from the top of the square tower." Hepzibah Pyncheon was to die as a witch on a place called Gallows Hill in Salem.[76]

The final scene is a deliberate parallel to the execution of Matthew Maule at the beginning of *The House of the Seven Gables*. But Hepzibah does not curse any of the Pyncheons. Still, it is very hard for Hepzibah to pray: ". . . she lifted her eyes—scowling, poor, dim-sighted Hepzibah, in the face of Heaven!—and strove hard to send up a prayer through the dense, gray pavement of clouds. Those mists had gathered, as if to symbolize a great, brooding mass of human trouble, doubt, confusion, and chill indifference. . . . Her faith was too weak; the prayer too heavy to be thus uplifted. It fell back, a lump of lead, upon her heart." Hepzibah's prayer on the isolated railroad platform at the end of the familiar version of "The Flight of Two Owls" is, in reality, her final petition:

> She knelt down upon the platform where they were standing, and lifted her clasped hands to the sky. The dull, gray weight of clouds made it invisible; but it was no hour for disbelief;—no juncture this, to question that there was a sky above, and an Almighty Father looking down from it!
>
> "Oh, God!"—ejaculated poor, gaunt Hepzibah—then paused a moment, to consider what her prayer should be—"Oh, God—our Father—are we not thy children? Have mercy on us!"[77]

Thus illustrated is Hawthorne's thesis that ". . . the wrong-doing of one generation lives into successive ones, and, divesting itself of every temporary advantage, becomes a pure and uncontrollable mischief. . . ."[78]

It is a fair conjecture what Hawthorne intended for the elusive Holgrave. This Maule, concealing his identity, comes to the House of the Seven Gables two months before Clifford arrives. Hepzibah, who "had gnashed her teeth against human law," senses a kindred lawless spirit in Holgrave and tells Phoebe, "I suppose he has a law of his own!"[79] Quite possibly Judge Pyncheon has sought the Maule out to be his key informer, believing that only that family could be vengeful enough to be trusted. But Holgrave, then, true to romantic convention, falls in love with Phoebe and abandons his scurrilous purposes. In a rare moment of honesty, he tells her that he lives in the ancient house "that I may know the better how to hate it."[80]

Quite aside from being an informer, Holgrave becomes surrounded by allusions to Shakespeare's *King Lear*. This tale of a family hopelessly divided by property and power offers a worthy parallel to the American story. Holgrave says, "I cannot help fancying that Destiny is arranging its fifth act for a catastrophe." He relates how his ancestor, Matthew Maule, was fabled to be able to regulate other people's dreams, "pretty much like the stage-manager of a theatre." Phoebe accuses Holgrave: "You talk as if this old house were a theatre; and you seem to look at Hepzibah's and Clifford's misfortunes, and those of generations before them, as a tragedy, such as I have seen acted in the hall of a country-hotel. . . ." And in commenting on the fall of the aristocratic Hepzibah to becoming the huckstress of a cent-shop, Hawthorne says: "The tragedy is enacted with as continual a repetition as that of a popular drama on a holiday, and, nevertheless, is felt as deeply, as when an hereditary noble sinks below his order."[81]

Hawthorne had attended Edmund Kean's performance of *King Lear* in Boston on March 5, 1820, and had written: "It was enough to have drawn tears from millstones. I could have cried myself if I had been in a convenient place for such an exploit." Reading Melville's article, "Hawthorne and His Mosses" in the August 7 and 24 issues of Duyckinck's *Literary World* thirty years later, Hawthorne must have recalled this performance: "Melville had been especially moved by Hawthorne's description of the orchard at the Old Manse and saw it, in an allegorical fashion, as 'the visible type of the fine mind that had described it.' In the stillness of summer afternoons, he, too, had heard the apples falling 'out of the mere necessity of perfect ripeness.' Having recently made a study of Shakespeare, Melville could hardly have failed to catch the echo of Lear's dictum, 'Ripeness is all.' "[82]

Nathaniel Hawthorne was ready to write about Salem, but the good citizens of Essex County and the politicos of that "unblessed" Custom House were not ready to appreciate Hawthorne's modern witch-hunt for Clifford and Hepzibah. The author concealed his true narrative, "to render it the more difficult of attainment" by the intolerant.[83] Hawthorne refers ironically to his own readers, directly, and to the possibility of the discovery of his deeper meaning and of his literary duplicity, or "proceedings": "Had any observer of these proceedings been aware of the fearful secret, hidden within the house, it would have affected him with a singular shape and modification of horror. . . ."[84]

Herman Melville held the literary key to unlock this secret treasure in *The House of the Seven Gables*. Inside the mansion he had found "a dark little black-letter volume in golden clasps, entitled 'Hawthorne: A Problem.' " Melville could not have given a more finely pointed hint to the people reading his review—a book within the book. To his credit, for his duplicity, Hawthorne made this explanation and public confession: "The better remedy is for the sufferer to pass on, and leave what he once thought his irreparable ruin far behind him."[85] It is likely that Hawthorne feared that his loss of the secure position at the Custom House, after years of struggle for financial stability for his growing family, would irreparably ruin him. This fear would account for his severe resentment of Salem politicians.

The drama's done. The legend of "The Sleeping Beauty" is a tale of promise, betrayal, loss, longing, and finally, the magnificent return of beauty. In *The House of the Seven Gables*, after the five-day storm, Phoebe returns from the country, just as she promised she would. One recalls the paradox that informs the lines by T. S. Eliot:

> The end of all our exploring
> will be to arrive where we started
> and know the place for the first time.
> Through the unknown, remembered gate.*[86]

For every return, there must be a recognition. The wandering exile Ulysses is cursed to roam, even after he has returned to his native land, until the oar—the symbol of his exile—appears to him to be a winnowing fan: that which removes the chaff from the wholesome grain.

By closely interpreting the universal meaning of "The Sleeping Beauty" that makes it endure, Nathaniel Hawthorne gave uncommon social depth to his isolated "characters" and local "types." His romance captures the mildness, the sunny, dappled light of a New Engand autumn afternoon: " 'He has *done* it,' said Oliver Wendell Holmes, 'and it will never be harsh country again. . . . A light falls upon the place not of land or sea! How much he did for Salem! Oh, the purple light, the soft haze, that now rests upon our glaring New England! He has *done* it, and it will never be harsh country again.' "[87]

*From "Little Gidding" in FOUR QUARTETS by T. S. Eliot, copyright 1943 by T. S. Eliot; renewed 1971 by Esme Valerie Eliot. Reprinted by permission of Harcourt Brace Jovanovich, Inc. Reprinted by permission of Faber and Faber Ltd. from FOUR QUARTETS by T. S. Eliot.

Notes

1. Nathaniel Hawthorne, *The House of the Seven Gables*, Vol. 2 of *The Centenary Edition of the Works of Nathaniel Hawthorne*, ed. Willliam Charvat, Roy Harvey Pearce, and Claude Simpson (Columbus, Ohio: Ohio State University Press, 1965), p. 2.
2. Letter to Evert A. Duyckinck, April 15, 1846, MS, Duyckinck Collection, The New York Public Library.

3. MS, Houghton Library, Harvard University. Hawthorne asks Longfellow in this letter for the best German grammar for beginning a study of the language.

4. The old Salem railroad station, built in 1847, was a castle. The president of the Eastern Railroad, after visiting English castles, drew sketches for it. It had two seventy-five–foot Gothic towers of gray Rockport granite, with seven tall, diamond-shaped paned windows between them. The trains emerged from a massive granite arch. Hawthorne describes ". . . the arched entrance of a large structure of gray stone. Within, there was a spacious breadth, and an airy height from floor to roof, now partially filled with smoke and steam" (*The House of the Seven Gables*, pp. 255–56). The castle references are from pp. 10, 271, 198, 65, and 229.

5. Hawthorne, *The House of the Seven Gables*, pp. 63, 257, 199, 204, 201.

6. The King's feast in "The Sleeping Beauty" is paralleled by an almost comical stress on food in the Seven Gables. The catalogue of viands at the Colonel's feast and at the political banquet for Judge Jaffrey, the feast planned by Uncle Venner for the neighborhood, and the "ogre-like appetite" of both Jaffrey and Clifford—especially the latter, at his mackeral breakfast—seem to indicate Hawthorne's appreciation of Sophia's cookery after the long "bachelorhood" diet.

7. Hawthorne, *The House of the Seven Gables*, Vol. 2, p. 2.

8. The child Gervayse runs toward the colonel, his grandfather, but stops, sensing death, and shrieks. This image of the child and the chair—without the presence of death—is favored by Hawthorne in "The Young Provincial," *The Universal History*, and *Grandfather's Chair*. He perhaps burlesques here the familiar old man in the fireside armchair. The Colonel's chair is also the death seat of Jaffrey Pyncheon two hundred years later. The skeleton at the feast is never far from Clifford's thoughts. He is described as one for whom life is ever "setting poison before them for a banquet."

9. Hawthorne, *The House of the Seven Gables*, p. 263.

10. Ibid., p. 20. Hawthorne never lived to see the day when the primary purpose of his nation's government was not to steal land from Indians and sell it as "real estate" or when black people were not subject to tax assessment—all with the utmost moral consent of the vast majority of his fellow citizens. The most barbaric and bitter conflicts in Hawthorne's time were over "property."

11. Ibid., p. 83.

12. Ibid., pp. 208, 205, 209.

13. Ibid., p. 212.

14. Ibid., pp. 213. 213–214. I am indebted to the magnificent and neglected meditation on the Sleeping Beauty legend titled, *Nostalgia: An Existential Exploration of Longing and Fulfillment in the Modern Age*, by Ralph Harper, with a foreword by Richard A. Macksey (Cleveland, Ohio: The Press of Western Reserve University, 1966).

15. Ibid., p. 71.

16. Ibid., p. 150.

17. Nathaniel Hawthorne, *Mosses from an Old Manse*, Vol. 10 of *The Centenary Edition* (Columbus, Ohio: Ohio State University Press, 1974), p. 217.

18. Ibid., pp. 180–181. From "The Hall of Fantasy."

19. Ibid., p. 181.

20. Hawthorne, *The House of the Seven Gables*, pp. 274,118.

21. Weeds, roses, and angels are common images in *The Scarlet Letter* and *The House of the Seven Gables*. The collective work that later became these two romances was intended to be called *Old-Time Legends: Together With Sketches, Experimental and Ideal*. Hester Prynne may be regarded as a kind of unfulfilled sleeping beauty, as she "might at any moment become a woman again, if there were only the magic touch to effect the transfiguration," Nathaniel Hawthorne, *The Scarlet Letter*, Vol. 1 of *The Centenary Edition*, [Columbus, Ohio: Ohio University Press, 1962], p. 182. In *Hawthorne, Melville and the Novel*, (Chicago, Illinois: University of Chicago Press, 1977), Richard Brodhead says that Hester, suffering Puritan censorship, seeks to "maintain all the elements of her true self in suspension. She cannot achieve in her life the full expression of her complex self that she has wrought into her symbol, but she instinctively and covertly moves to keep this alive as a possibility." In order to protect her repressed passion, "Once so wild, and even yet neither dead nor asleep," Hester rejects anything that might soothe it (p. 62). This includes, in the chapter "Hester at Her Needle," her own elaborate embroidery, which she comes to regard as too pleasurable and sinful. And in "Hester and Pearl," she rejects any possibility of using her daughter as a friend and confidante when she tells Pearl, falsely, that she wears the scarlet letter for the sake of its gold-embroidered thread. But Hester is condemned to remain a sleeping beauty, with no true awakening. This may well be because Nathaniel Hawthorne intended *The Scarlet Letter* to be a highly literary murder mystery along the lines indicated in Dr. Jemshed A. Khan's convincing article "Atropine Poisoning in Hawthorne's *The Scarlet Letter*" (The *New England Journal of Medicine*, August 9, 1984, 311: 414–16).

22. Hawthorne, *The House of the Seven Gables*, pp. 68, 73, 86, 72. This hedge-of-thorns image persisted throughout later works. In his "Preface To Horatio Bridge, Esq., U.S.N.," Hawthorne says: "I sat down by the wayside of life, like a man under enchantment, and a shrubbery sprung up around me, and the bushes grew to be saplings, and the saplings became trees, until no exit appeared possible, through the entangling depths of my obscurity" (*The Snow-Image and Uncollected Tales*, Vol. 11 of *The Centenary Edition* [Columbus, Ohio: University of Ohio Press, 1974], p. 5). Hawthorne usually associated the word *entangle* with this hedge of thorns—hence the "tanglewood," his name for the immense thicket that blocked the path to

the lake in the Berkshire Hills called the Stockbridge Bowl. He describes the labyrinthine maze of hedge-bordered walks in the Jephson Garden at Leamington Spa in England as a "sad emblem of the mental and moral perplexities in which we sometimes go astray, petty in scope, yet large enough to entangle a lifetime, and bewilder us with a weary movement, but no genuine progress" (Nathaniel Hawthorne, *Our Old Home: A Series of English Sketches*, Vol. 5 of *The Centenary Edition*, [Columbus, Ohio: University of Ohio Press, 1970], p. 45.) In *Doctor Grimshawe's Secret*, Hawthorne describes, elaborately, a hedge of "green intricacy," and "impenetrable . . . labyrinth of little boughs and twigs, unseen and inaccessible." *(The American Claimaint Manuscripts*, Vol. 12 of *The Centenary Edition* [Columbus: The Ohio State University Press, 1977], p. 442).

23. Hawthorne, *The House of the Seven Gables*, pp. 91, 84, 86, 181.

24. Ibid., p. 177.

25. Ibid., p. 180.

26. Louise Hall Tharp, *The Peabody Sisters of Salem* (Boston: Little, Brown and Company, 1950), pp. 162–163, 350n.

27. Hawthorne did not intend his readers to be fully aware of the presence of the legend of the Sleeping Beauty in *The House of the Seven Gables*. He makes a literary secret of his sources. In the late romance, *Doctor Grimshawe's Secret*, one secret lies in the title itself. It holds two allusions—to the brothers Grimm, and to the author himself. Thus Grimms plus Hawthorne equals Grimshawe. It is also Doctor Grimshawe, because Jakob and Wilhelm were fully accredited academics—professors of philology. Doctor Grimshawe lives near the fictional counterpart to the Charter Street burying ground, and the children Ned and Elsie, we are told, sometimes have their "graver" moods while playing there. Hawthorne strikes another pun in referring to "grim Doctor Grimshawe" and later repeatedly calls his character by the attenuated name Doctor Grim. It will be recalled that Hawthorne's first novel was titled *Fanshawe*. The protagonist Fanshawe was inspired by the author's admiration for one Gorham Deane, a fellow student at Bowdoin who, like Nathaniel Mather, died young—another "hard student." Fanshawe or Grimshawe, Hawthorne had an undeniably playful turn on occasion. One droll moment gives Doctor Grimshawe a blackened, foul-smelling old German pipe.

28. Robert Cantwell, *Nathaniel Hawthorne: The American Years* (New York: Octagon Books, 1979), p. 237.

29. Tharp, *The Peabody Sisters*, p. 38. Smaller doses, given more often.

30. Julian Hawthorne, *Hawthorne and His Wife: A Biography* (Boston, Massachusetts: Houghton, Mifflin and Company, 1884), pp. 63, 64, 78.

31. Ibid., pp. 54–55.

32. Tharp, *The Peabody Sisters*, p. 77.

33. Hawthorne, *Hawthorne and His Wife*, p. 67. Sophia Peabody's maternal uncle was Royall Tyler, famed author of the stage comedy *The Contrast*

(1787), which compared the British and the Americans.
34. Tharp, *The Peabody Sisters*, p. 103.
35. Love Letters, August 18, 1841.
36. Cantwell, *Nathaniel Hawthorne*, p. 290.
37. Hubert H. Hoeltje, *The Inward Sky: The Mind and Heart of Nathaniel Hawthorne* (Durham, North Carolina: Duke University Press, 1962), p. 191.
38. Nathaniel Hawthorne, *Tales, Sketches and Other Papers by Nathaniel Hawthorne*, Vol. 12 of *Hawthorne's Works*, with a biographical sketch by George Parsons Lathrop (Boston and New York: Houghton, Mifflin and Company, The Riverside Press, Cambridge, 1883), p. 25. From the sketch "Journal of a Solitary Man."
39. Hawthorne, *The House of the Seven Gables*, p. 112.
40. Hawthorne, *Hawthorne and His Wife*. Julian Hawthorne cites his father's letter to Sophia.
41. Arlin Turner, *Nathaniel Hawthorne; A Biography* (New York and Oxford: Oxford University Press, 1980), pp. 208–209.
42. Hawthorne may have first thought of Salem as another Troy during the War of 1812, with the arrival of the British (Greek) fleet. Eight years old in that year, Nathaniel had been sent away for safety, protesting that he wished to see the enemy arrive. The child was proud that his father had led the *Herald* and four American ships in an attack on a French privateer throughout two days in November 1800, thus saving a British ship.
43. Hawthorne, *The House of the Seven Gables*, p. 40. The phrase may be Hawthorne's own translation of that bellwether for Latin scholars *"discolor unde auri per ramos aura refulsit."* The twin doves leading Aeneas alight on a tree holding the Golden Bough.
44. Ibid., p. 57.
45. Ibid., p. 285.
46. Rolfe Humphries, *The Aeneid of Virgil: A Verse Translation* (New York: Charles Scribner's Sons, 1951), p. 153. Book 6 of the *Aeneid*, in which Aeneas visits his ghostly ancestors in the Lower World and envisions his descendants, is echoed in Hawthorne's midnight gathering of the Pyncheon clan and by Maule's Well, which "fore-shadowed the coming fortunes of Hepzibah, and Clifford, and the descendant of the legendary wizard, and the village-maiden over whom he had thrown love's web of sorcery" (Hawthorne, *The House of the Seven Gables*, p. 319).
47. The "golden bough" found on the oak tree is so named because it bears the parasitic mistletoe, which blooms unexpectedly in the dead of winter. In *Doctor Grimshawe's Secret*, Hawthorne observes that "on one venerable oak there was a plant of mystic leaf which the traveller knew by instinct, and plucked a bough of it with a certain reverence for the sake of the Druids . . . and of the poetry in which it was rooted from of old" (*Tales*, p. 443). The "poetry" alluded to is most likely Virgil's *Aeneid*. The inscru-

table Doctor Grimshawe utters dreadful curses that:

> seemed to have produced a very remarkable [effect] on the unfortunate elm tree, through the naked branches of which the Doctor discharged this fiendish shot. For, the next spring, when April came, no tender leaves budded forth, no life awakened there; and never again, on that old elm, widely as its roots were imbedded among the dead of many years, was there rustling bough in the summer time, or the elm's early golden boughs in September; and after waiting till another spring to give it a fair chance of reviving, it was cut down and made into coffins, and burnt on the sexton's hearth. The general opinion was that the grim Doctor's awful profanity had blasted that tree, fostered, as it had been, on grave-mould of Puritans.

48. Hawthorne, *The House of the Seven Gables*, p. 142. The Roman people considered the Islands of the Blest to be Paradise. Appropos of the *Aeneid*, Hawthorne often alludes to Roman history. The worshipful Gervayse Pyncheon owns a black man whom he calls Scipio, after Scipio Africanus Major, the successful general in the war against Carthage. Clifford's memory is like the wheel tracks of ancient vehicles in Herculaneum, the resort for the rich that was buried under volcanic ash by the eruption of Vesuvius in A.D. 79. Clifford is called a Sybarite, after the rich, indulgent, pleasure-loving people of Sybaris, the first Greek colony founded on the Gulf of Taranto in southern Italy. The imaginary "tutelary Lar" in the Seven Gables was an Etruscan and Roman guardian spirit of the home. Hepzibah heaves sighs like those heard in the Cave of Aeolus (god of the winds). Gervayse Pyncheon has in his study an Italian landscape by the French painter Claude Lorrain.
49. Ibid., pp. 182–83. In Roman mythology, Charon will not ferry over the Styx the spirit of any person that has not been properly buried. Such are doomed to wander hopelessly on the shore for 100 years.
50. Hawthorne, *Tales, Doctor Grimshawe's Secret*.
51. *Hawthorne's Works*, p. 26.
52. Tharp, *The Peabody Sisters*, pp. 6–9
53. Hawthorne, *The House of the Seven Gables*, p. 253.
54. Ibid., pp. 313, 64, 38.
55. Bernard M. W. Knox, "The Serpent and the Flame: The Imagery of the Second Book of the *Aeneid*" in *Virgil: A Collection of Critical Essays*, ed. Steele Commager (Englewood Cliffs, New Jersey: Prentice-Hall, Inc., 1966), pp. 124–42.
56. Hawthorne, *The House of the Seven Gables*, pp. 216, 119, 162.
57. Hawthorne's letter to Horace Conolly, June 17, 1850, Bowdoin (transcript). Cited by James R. Mellow, pp. 319–320. (See note 70.)
58. Letter to Evert A. Duyckinck, April 27, 1851, MS, Duyckinck Collection, New York Public Library.
59. Hawthorne, *The Scarlet Letter*, p. 271.
60. Letter to James A. Fields, November 29, 1850, MS, Collection of

Norman Holmes Pearson.

61. MS, The Berg Collection, The New York Public Library. On January 27, 1851, Sophia wrote: ". . . 'The House of the Seven Gables' was finished yesterday. Mr. Hawthorne read me the close, last evening. There is unspeakable grace and beauty in the conclusion, throwing back upon the sterner tragedy of the commencement an ethereal light, and a dear home-loveliness and satisfaction. How you will enjoy the book,—and its depth of wisdom, its high tone, the flowers of Paradise scattered over all the dark places. . . ."

62. That intelligent reader of *The House of the Seven Gables*, Herman Melville knew "that it was not to be taken literally and simply, but had a hidden process involved in it that made the whole thing infinitely deeper than he had hitherto deemed it to be. Indeed, it appeared to him, on close observation, that it had not been the intention of the writer really to conceal what he had written from any earnest student, but rather to lock it up for safety in a sort of coffer, of which diligence and insight should be the key, and the keen intelligence with which the meaning was sought should be the test of the seeker's being entitled to possess the secret treasure." With these two sentences, Hawthorne ostensibly describes his protagonist, Septimius Felton, at the moment he discovers that the mysterious manuscript before him "was part of that secret writing for which the Age of Elizabeth was so famous and so dexterous." *The Dolliver Romance, Fanshawe, Septimius Felton*, with an Appendix containing *The Ancestral Footstep* by Nathaniel Hawthorne, Vol. 11 of *Hawthorne's Works* [Boston and New York: Houghton, Mifflin, and Company; The Riverside Press, Cambridge, 1883], pp. 337, 397. Melville never betrayed Hawthorne's confidence. In 1883 Julian Hawthorne visited Melville in New York City, on East Twenty-sixth, "a quiet side street . . . where he was living almost alone," and asked for any of his father's letters—for a biography he was writing of his parents. Melville replied with a melancholy gesture that they "had all been destroyed long since . . . that he had kept nothing." Asked to recall the red-cottage days, Melville only shook his head. Almost twenty years after Nathaniel's death, Julian describes his old friend: "He seemed nervous, and every few minutes would rise to open and then to shut again the window opening on the court yard. . . . He was convinced Hawthorne had all his life concealed some great secret, which would, were it known, explain all the mysteries of his career . . . some secret in my father's life which had never been revealed, and which accounted for the gloomy passages in his books. It was characteristic in him to imagine so; there were many secrets untold in his own career." (Alfred Kazin, *An American Procession* (New York: Alfred A. Knopf, 1984), pp. 148–49.

63. Hawthorne, *The House of the Seven Gables*, pp. 247–48 and following.

64. Ibid., pp. 165–66.

65. Melville felt that Hawthorne's portrait of Clifford was "full of an awful truth throughout."

66. Hawthorne, *The House of the Seven Gables*, pp. 291, 309.

67. Herman Melville, *Moby-Dick; or, The Whale*, edited with an introduction and annotations by Charles Feidelson, Jr. (Indianapolis, Indiana: The Bobbs-Merrill Company, Inc., 1964), p. 724. Hawthorne had compared Judge Pyncheon to that unpleasant mortal in Greek mythology, Ixion.

68. Hawthorne, *The House of the Seven Gables*, p. 230.

69. Nathaniel Hawthorne, *Our Old Home: A Series of English Sketches*, Vol. 5 of *The Centenary Edition* (Columbus: The Ohio State University Press, 1970).

70. Hawthorne, *The House of the Seven Gables*, pp. 40, 126. Clifford sleeps in the parlor. His character is that of an overgrown child, apparently modeled on an earlier character, Ilbrahim, the Quaker child in "The Gentle Boy." Clifford resembles "his mother; and she, a lovely and loveable woman, with perhaps some beautiful infirmity of character, that made it all the pleasanter to know, and easier to love her" (p. 60). Hepzibah thinks, "They persecuted his mother in him! He never was a Pyncheon!" Hawthorne was aware that his ancestor William Hathorne had helped to smite the Quaker heretics. Critic James R. Mellow notes that Melville underlined a passage in "The Gentle Boy" and later echoed it with his dramatic opening "Call me Ishmael": " 'Friend,' replied the little boy in a sweet though faltering voice, 'they call me Ilbrahim and my home is here.' " The boy is weeping by his father's grave, this man having suffered execution by the Puritan judges. (James R. Mellow, *Nathaniel Hawthorne in His Times* [Boston: Houghton Mifflin Company, 1980], p. 354).

71. Ibid., pp. 42, 49.

72. Ibid., pp. 48–49. Satan's city is most likely the Temple Place part of Boston, near West Street and Tremont Street, and that area between the Boston Common and the Park Street Church that was once known as Brimstone Corner.

73. Ibid., pp. 33–34, 223–24, 41, 47, 288–89.

74. Ibid., pp. 236, 289, 296.

75. Ibid., pp. 291–92.

76. Ibid., pp. 264, 253, 255, 256, 266.

77. Ibid., pp. 245, 267. One fragment, "Indeed, she had not energy to fling it down, but only ceased to uphold it, and suffered it to press her to the earth," may reveal Hepzibah's manner of execution—slow pressing to death beneath a board or plank, upon which heavy stones are gradually piled. The very elderly Giles Corey in Salem in 1692 was executed in this manner, crying out in the end continually for "More weight! More weight!" to break his rib cage and end the agony.

78. Ibid., from the preface, p. 2.

79. Ibid., p. 85.

80. Ibid., p. 184.

81. Ibid., pp. 218, 189, 217, 38.

82. James R. Mellow, *Nathaniel Hawthorne in His Times*, p. 334.

83. Hawthorne, *The House of the Seven Gables*, from the preface, p. 2.
84. Ibid., p. 291.
85. Ibid., p. 313.
86. T. S. Eliot, *The Complete Poems and Plays 1909–1950* (New York: Harcourt, Brace and Company, 1952), p. 145.
87. Rose Hawthorne Lathrop, *Memories of Hawthorne* (Boston: Houghton Mifflin, 1887).

3

Jonathan Edwards Rebukes the New York Negro Rebels: "Sinners in the Hands of An Angry God"

You gave
her Pompey, a Negro slave,
and eleven children.
Yet people were spiders
in your moment of glory,
at the Great Awakening—"Alas, how many
in this very meeting house are more than likely
*to remember my discourse in hell!"**

—Robert Lowell

"Sinners in the Hands of an Angry God," delivered in Enfield, Connecticut, on July 8, 1741, is a jeremiad against the black slaves and freemen who were then on trial in New York City, accused of plotting to burn that village down and murder all its white citizens. This famed hellfire-and-brimstone "spider" sermon is not merely zealous and irresponsible Calvinism unleashed, but a very topical work—Edwards's direct response to the lurid events in the colony to the south. Considering the black men to be guilty as charged, Edwards, in text, theme, and unforgettable imagery, warns his congre-

* Excerpt from "Jonathan Edwards in Western Massachusetts" reprinted by permission of Farrar, Straus and Giroux, Inc. from FOR THE UNION DEAD by Robert Lowell. Copyright © 1962, 1964 by Robert Lowell.

gation to witness and fear the divine retribution rendered to rebels. If there were any Negroes in the gallery, the sermon was directed especially to them.[2]

During the peak of the Great Awakening, the Protestant stronghold of New York suffered a hysteria similar to that which had seized Salem Village in 1692, two generations before.[3] The suspected "Negro Plot," as it came to be called, resulted in the most brutal excesses of the Awakening: from May to August 1741, thirteen slaves were tried, sentenced, and burned at the stake in the public marketplace—"a grassy valley" located at the present-day conjunction of Baxter, Worth, and Park Streets, just behind the New York County Courthouse. Eighteen slaves were hanged—two in chains—and seventy-two were transported to the West Indies, which meant an all-but-certain death.[4]

Considered historically, the hysteria was entirely creditable. New Yorkers knew that slave rebellions could be successful at times. Of their population of eleven thousand, over two thousand were black or Indian. Observers of the "Bloody Tragedy" that summer compared the events to the town's 1712 black uprising, which had left eight or ten white citizens dead. Twenty-one slaves had then been executed: "Some were burnt, others hanged, one broke on the wheel, and one hung alive in chains in the town." Some were roasted over a slow fire, tormented for up to ten hours before death.[5] Moreover, the Charleston, South Carolina, area had suffered three separate insurrections in 1739, quite formidable ones. Early in May 1741, eight miles away from New York, in Hackensack, New Jersey, two black slaves had been burned alive at the stake for setting fire to seven barns. An eighth barn "was three times endeavoured to be served the same; but happily escaped . . . saved by the diligence of the Neighbors" but the alarm was sufficient to make New Yorkers "keep under Arms every Night." The *New England Weekly Journal* for May 12, 1741, reported that "it is said, the first Day of this Month was the Time appointed for New York to be burnt."[6] There had been an unexplained succession of fires in recent weeks. The village structures were mostly wood, and rumors of slave rebellion could develop easily. Fear rippled throughout New England. In June, a black slave was burned in Albany, New York, charged with child murder.[7] Racial fears spurred the conversions and convulsions of the Great Awakening.

When the "Negro Plot" had finally seemed to have run its course, the hysteria burst forth again, newly christened as the "Papist Plot." The incendiary blacks, it was held, were directed by white Catholic spies. This notion was entirely creditable, given the circumstances. Spain was at war with England, and the fear was that Catholics disguised as school-teachers and dancing masters were plotting to burn New York in order to prevent the British fleet from using its harbor for attacks on Spanish shipping in the West Indies. Catholic spies were also reportedly inciting the black slaves to flee to freedom among the French Jesuits in Canada. It was known that during the recent rebellion in South Carolina, Cato and his band had been marching toward freedom in Saint Augustine, then under Spanish Catholic hegemony. Even during peacetime, it was a capital offense for any priest to enter the precincts of New York. The Great Awakening demanded a Catholic to sacrifice for its own rebirth.

An innocent itinerant schoolteacher and Latinist—one John Ury—recently arrived in New York, an Anglican, well traveled, with an unfortunate love for theological dispute, was arrested for having been seen in the same tavern with some of the executed blacks and put on trial. A fellow schoolteacher superficially acquainted with Ury testified as to his religious beliefs. This testimony reveals, incidentally, how closely racial and religious fears were linked: "Another time at my school, I had some discourse with him concerning Mr. Whitefield's letter in answer to Mr. Wesley's sermon on free-grace, which letter he did not approve of at all, and told me he believed it was through the great encouragement the negroes had received from Mr. Whitefield, we had all the disturbance, and that he believed Mr. Whitefield was more of a Roman than anything else, and he believed he came abroad with no good design. . . ."[8] The prosecuting lawyers took this as an attack on the popular English revivalist preacher George Whitefield, who was prominent in the Great Awakening and had recently toured America. John Ury was hanged for the crime of inciting black slaves to burn New York City. To pious Protestants everywhere, mindful of the spectacle of Sodom and Gomorrah, the destruction, by fire, of a wicked city seemed entirely creditable, with black slaves as the agents of an angry vengeful God. Prominent ministers knew that such fears and suspicions had to be controlled by direct speech.

Jonathan Edwards's best friend from his youth at Yale and from his first pastorate in New York City, from 1722 to 1723, was one John Smith—the main prosecuting lawyer in the "Negro Plot" trials. John Smith's father, Thomas, was a trustee of the splinter group from the First Presbyterian Church on Wall Street. Edwards preached to this congregation and paid his rent to Madam Thomas Smith. The lonely Jonathan Edwards had finally

> . . . found a friend, John Smith, a member of his congregation and of the household in which he lived. This was not a friendship which brought new interests. John Smith . . . was apparently a simple person who supplied no new stimulus whatever, the only basis for companionship between the boys being their pleasure in reading their Bibles, walking in the woods, and talking together about the "things of religion"; but this was quite enough. For Jonathan Edwards the sharing of such joys was a completely new experience. It was also of more than transient importance. Twenty years later he was still receiving letters from "my dear friend Mr. John Smith of York."[9]

Lawyer John Smith delivered flights of high-minded religious rhetoric to his juries; his harangues at the black slaves in the dock brought sentences of death. The trials opened with the prosecution raging against the Papists, the Spanish Inquisition, the Saint Bartholomew's massacre, the Gunpowder Plot of Guy Fawkes in 1605, and the atrocities of the duke of Alva in the Netherlands. In Smith's tirades lie the darker side of the Great Awakening:

> . . . the monstrous wickedness of this plot would prob-
> ably among strangers impeach its credit; but if it be
> considered as the contrivance of the public enemy, and
> the inhuman dictate of a bloody religion, the wonder
> ceases.
>
> What more cruel and unnatural can be conceived,
> than what Rome had contrived; yea what more savage
> and barbarous, than what popery has attempted, and
> sometimes executed, for the extirpation of that which
> the papists call heresy? We need not go so far from home
> as the vallies [sic] of Piedmont, nor rake into the ashes
> of the ancient Waldenses and Albigenses, for tragical
> instances of popish cruelty. We need not remind you of
> the massacre at Paris, not the later desolations in France,
> nor mention the horrible slaughters of the duke d'Alva,
> in the Low Countries. We need not recount the many
> millions of lives, that in remote countries, and different
> ages, have been sacrificed to the Roman idol; nor meas-
> ure out to you that ocean of foreign blood with which
> the scarlet whore hath made herself perpetually drunk.[10]

The darker side of the Great Awakening is apparent in
this slightly out-of-control rhetoric; it is immeasurably more
concealed in the perfect style and structure of the topical
sermon "Sinners in the Hands of an Angry God." Control is,
indeed, of the essence for Jonathan Edwards, in his complete
terror at the slave revolt's assault on the divine order and the
king of England. An anachronism in his own time, Edwards
was the last major American colonial thinker to absorb medieval concepts without the taint of democratic theorizings
about "the rights of man." Crippled by a penchant for social
conformity and orthodoxy in all things, with a noticeably excessive respect for authority per se, Edwards shackled his
logically sophisticated, occasionally poetical intelligence in the
prison house of Calvinist theology. He was happiest in elu-

cidating the beauty, the harmony and magnificence, the virtue and light of his God's universe. When he did adopt the hell-fire-and-brimstone manner, it was to prod reluctant people into realizing their possibilities.

The great, constricting conservative in Jonathan Edwards forced the man to accept the church's traditional rationalizations and obfuscations in favor of the American slave trade. Elegant Scriptural exegeses illuminated the essential Christianity of converting and convincing those "most Bruitish of Creatures upon Earth," the black slaves, of the beneficence of the white race. In 1706, Cotton Mather stressed conversion as the most useful tool for quelling rebellious instincts: "The greatest Kindness that can be done to any Man is to make a Christian of him. Your Negroes are immediately Raised unto an astonishing Felicity, when you have Christianized them. They are become amiable spectacles, & such as the Angels of God would gladly repair unto the Windows of Heaven to look upon."

Before the Revolution, if the New England clergy had any scruples about stealing African men, they could be numbed by appeals to the logic of Cotton Mather. Should this fail to charm, the recollection of last Sabbath's generous contribution in the offering plate by prominent local slave merchants would suffice. In 1706, his congregation presented Cotton Mather with a slave worth fifty pounds sterling. The minister duly recorded the profit as "a smile from Heaven."[11] The New England clergy dreaded slave rebellion as an immediate threat to their property rights. It is entirely creditable, then, that in 1723, when Boston was disturbed by a series of fires "purposely set by ye Negroes," the Rev. Joseph Sewall preached a special sermon and emergency laws were passed severely punishing any Negroes caught near a fire.[12]

There was simply nothing in Jonathan Edwards's epistemology capable of generating a concept of a "victim." For the minister and his friend John Smith, the black men tortured and executed in New York were merely heathen African ingrates, blasphemously impervious to their own chances to enjoy a Gospel dispensation in a new Christian land. Even now, Smith's conservative obfuscations have a familiar ring: "Gentlemen, the monstrous ingratitude of this black tribe is what exceedingly aggravates their guilt. Their slavery among us is generally softened with great indulgence, they live without care, and are commonly better fed and clothed, and put to less labour, than the poor of most Christian countries. They are indeed slaves, but under the protection of the law, none can hurt them with impunity: they are really more happy in this place. . . ."[13]

Before the "Negro Plot," New York held only happy memories for Edwards. It was the scene of his original religious conversion, on January 12, 1723, when he was filled with awe for the words in I Timothy 1:17—"Now unto the King eternal, immortal, invisible, the only wise God, be honour and glory for ever and ever." This revelation was soon followed by his seventy *Resolutions*. There was time for contemplative strolls in the forests along the Hudson River. In a few months, Edwards sailed for New England, after "a most bitter parting with Madam Smith and her son," and later he would write: "My Heart seemed to sink within me at leaving the family and City where I had enjoyed so many sweet and pleasant Days." Soon he was to marry Sarah Pierrepont, whose maternal great-grandfather had been Thomas Willet, the first mayor of New York City. Jonathan Edwards never severed his connections with that British colony.

The news from New York in the summer of 1741 must have stirred long-forgotten memories in Edwards: slaves laughing and talking by the wells, the town pumps, and the tea-water reservoirs—these being the only places that slaves could congregate in any significant numbers without violating the laws. Surely the slave market and auction on Wall Street must have attracted his attention. Perhaps also there were less pleasant incidents recalled, unexpectedly and unwelcomely. Brooding, then, over the "Negro Plot" scenes of agony taking place at the sweet scene of his youth and first stirrings of faith, Edwards composed "Sinners in the Hands of an Angry God." The sermon describes the executions graphically. It is certain that Edwards imagined himself in the place of his fellow ministers in New York, whose duty it was to officiate at the stake.[14]

Recalling Deuteronomy 32, the book of the law in which Moses confronts the "perverse and crooked generation," Edwards imagined the failed attempts of the rebels and chose his text: verse 35, "Their foot shall slide in due time." Then he began: "In this verse is threatened the vengeance of God on the wicked unbelieving Israelites, who were God's visible people, and who lived under the means of grace; but who, notwithstanding all God's wonderful works towards them, remained [as verse 28] void of counsel, having no understanding in them. Under all the cultivations of Heaven, they brought forth bitter and poisonous fruit.[15] The expression "void of counsel" here refers to the fact that not one lawyer in New York came forward to defend the slaves.[16]

Yet the thought of black men chained to the stakes in the public marketplace, surrounded by wood piled high to consume them, amid the screaming populace, must have disturbed Edwards, a man of aesthetic and delicate sensibilities. The minister deals with his shock and outrage in unforgettable imagery:

> . . . The wrath of God burns against them, their damnation does not slumber; the pit is prepared, the fire is made ready, the furnace is now hot, ready to receive them; the flames do now rage and glow. . . .
> . . . The corruption of the heart of man is immoderate and boundless in its fury; and while wicked men live here, it is like fire pent up by God's restraints, whereas if it were let loose, it would set on fire the course of nature; and as the heart is now a sink of sin, so, if sin was not restrained, it would immediately turn the soul into a fiery oven, or a furnace of fire and brimstone.

Edwards's repeated and nightmarish stress on the sinner

standing on a shaky platform and dangling over hell are graphic images of black slaves at the moment just before they are hanged. Ministers in New York stood by unconfessed, unrepentant, or defiant blacks, exhorting them to admit their guilt. Usually they did not. Some had the audacity to protest their innocence to the last: Edwards exhorted: "O sinner! Consider the fearful danger you are in: it is a great furnace of wrath. . . . You hang by a slender thread, with the flames of divine wrath flashing about it, and ready every moment to singe it, and burn it asunder; and you have no interest in any Mediator, and nothing to lay hold of to save yourself, nothing to keep off the flames of wrath, nothing of your own, nothing that you ever have done, nothing that you can do, to induce God to spare you one moment."

The sheriff of New York released the scaffold trap so frequently that summer that Jonathan Edwards almost naturally describes and threatens a physical fall to perdition: "Their foot shall slide in due time," the thought of him "that walks in slippery places," and the unconverted who "walk over the pit of hell on a rotten covering," and the vision "that natural men are held in the hand of God, over the pit of hell." Then there is that grotesque and pitiless, apocalyptic image of the drama between the Creator and his creature, man:

> The God that holds you over the pit of hell, much as one holds a spider, or some loathsome insect, over the fire, abhors you, and is dreadfully provoked; his wrath towards you burns like fire; he looks upon you as worthy of nothing else, but to be cast into the fire; he is of purer eyes than to bear to have you in his sight; you are ten thousand times more abominable in his eyes, than the most hateful venemous serpent is in ours. You have offended him infinitely more than ever a stubborn rebel did his prince: and yet, it is nothing but his hand that holds you from falling into the fire every moment. It is to be ascribed to nothing else, that you did not go to hell the last night; that you were suffered to wake again in

this world, after you closed your eyes to sleep. And there is no other reason to be given, why you have not dropped into hell since you arose in the morning, but that God's hand has held you up. There is no other reason to be given why you have not gone to hell, since you have sat here in the house of God, provoking his pure eyes by your sinful wicked manner of attending his solemn worship. Yea, there is nothing else that is to be given as a reason why you do not this very moment drop down into hell.

Edwards plays frequently on the racial fears of the frontier settlers in Connecticut, especially with their memories of Indian uprisings. Verses 23 and 42 of Deuteronomy 32—"I will spend mine arrows upon them," and "I will make mine arrows drunk with blood"—appear in this sermon: "The bow of God's wrath is bent, and the arrow made ready on the string, and justice bends the arrow at your heart, and strains the bow, and it is nothing but the mere pleasure of God, and that of an angry God, without any promise or obligation at all, that keeps the arrow one moment from being made drunk with your blood." The congregation is also informed that "the arrows of death fly unseen at noonday; the sharpest sight cannot discern them."

But the minister guiltily returns to the execution theme he cannot forget with an adaptation of Deuteronomy 32:41, "The glittering sword is whet; and held over them, and the pit hath opened its mouth under them"; Isaiah 16:15, "For behold, the Lord will come with fire, and with his chariots like a whirlwind, to render his anger with fury, and his rebuke with flames of fire"; and Isaiah 33:12–14, "And the people shall be as the burnings of lime, as thorns cut up shall they be burnt in the fire. Hear ye, that are far off, what I have done and ye that are near, acknowledge my might."

Edwards apparently equated political rebellion with religious heresy. In "The Artistry of Jonathan Edwards," Edwin H. Cady notes that "the theme of righteous king against rebellious subject is significantly used four times, including once as a sub-strand of the spider metaphor and again as the key to the whole section 1 of the 'Application.' "[17] Edward's friendship with the lawyer John Smith could only have inclined him toward the notion that there was something inherently sacrosanct about state authority.

Robert Lowell accuses Jonathan Edwards of a surprising lack of noblesse oblige in depicting people as spiders. The image of the black spider shriveling up in the inferno was, however, unknown to Robert Lowell, a representation of a black slave being burned at the stake. Robert Lowell clearly cannot be faulted for missing the connection. The entire background of the "Negro Plot," so necessary to any understanding of "Sinners in the Hands of an Angry God," has been conveniently forgotten long ago and is deliberately kept so, in the interests of putting a happy face on slavery.[18] But the cultural memory of the facts survives in the legend of Jonathan Edwards as a predominantly hellfire-and-brimstone preacher, which he was not. This is a case of poetic justice.

Edwards did not create horrifying visions of torture in order to hurl his own people into despair. The congregation, unwilling to accept the moral responsibility for slavery and its trade, needed "Sinners in the Hands of an Angry God" to allay, or relieve, the sharp pangs of conscience provoked by the events in New York. Although the people in Enfield "yelled and shrieked, they rolled in the aisles, they crowded up into the pulpit and begged him to stop," forcing the minister at one point to "speak to the people and desire silence, that he might be heard," still, the congregation knew what it wanted: a numbed conscience.

Seizing the congregation with terror and working them to the pitch of panic, Edwards then reassured the elect and glided into a composed and hopeful conclusion. The skilled revivalist preacher makes a direct and moving appeal to the unrepentant sinner to seek again the better way: "Now God stands ready to pity you; this is a day of mercy; you may cry now with some encouragement of obtaining mercy." Edwards chides the sore-distressed: "What would not those poor damned hopeless souls give for the day's opportunity such as you now enjoy!" He speaks of the Great Awakening itself: "God seems now to be hastily gathering in his elect in all parts of the land; and probably the greater part of adult persons that ever shall be saved, will be brought in now in a little time." Edwards then makes a final appeal to the unconverted, referring to Genesis 19:17 and fiery Sodom and Gomorrah: "Haste and escape for your lives, look not behind you, escape to the mountain, lest you be consumed."

The citizens of Enfield, Connecticut, were indeed deeply satisfied with "Sinners in the Hands of an Angry God." Stephen Williams records this content:

> We went over to Enfl___where we met dear M^r E___of N___ H___who preach^d a most awakening sermon from these words—Deut. 32–35 and before sermon was done—there was a great moaning & crying out through ye whole House—What Shall I do to be Sav^d—oh I am going to Hell—Oh what shall I do for Christ &c.&c. So y^t ye minister was obliged to desist—ye shrieks & cry^s were piercing & Amazing—after Some time of waiting the Congregation were Still so y^t a prayer was made by Mr W. & after that we descen^d from the pulpitt and discours^d with the people—Some in one place and Some in another—and Amazing and Astonishing ye power of God was seen—Several souls were hopefully wrought upon y^t night. & oh ye cheerfulness and pleasantness of their countenances y^t receiv^d comfort—oh y^t God wd strengthen and confirm—we sung an hymn & pray^d & dismiss^d ye Assembly.[19]

The Enfield congregation was jubilant, but thrilling sermons in Connecticut could be no solace to slaves in New York City. Before the overthrow of the British government, colonial clergymen like Jonathan Edwards seldom, if ever, felt impelled to reconcile the practice of slavery with Christian ethics. This was beneath their dignity. Indeed, the Divinity was often perceived as *abetting* the work of slaughter. When one John Van Zandt of New York City horsewhipped his slave to death for having violated the curfew in 1735, the coroner's jury handed in the verdict that "the correction given by the master was not the Cause of his [the slave's] Death, but that it was by the Visitation of God." Such are the hidden snares of militant and missionary Christianity.

Notes

1. Robert Lowell, *For the Union Dead* (New York: Farrar, Straus and Giroux, Inc., 1965), p. 42.
2. There is a tradition that Edwards stared fixedly at the bell rope all through his sermon. This rigid delivery was noticeable because most uncharacteristic. The bell rope hangs down directly in front of the pulpit. It is possible that Edwards was not looking at the rope itself, but beyond it, to the gallery where the black servants listened.
3. The prominent New Yorker Cadwallader Colden received an anonymous letter from the province of Massachusetts Bay, probably Boston, on July 8, 1741, enclosed in another letter from his daughter DeLancey. Penned at the moment when the chief accuser in the trials, one Mary Burton, was reimbursed for her services (100 pounds sterling) and taken away quickly when she began to accuse the highest and most unimpeachable authorities in the city, the writer cynically notes that a parallel development had "finished our Salem Witchcraft." This writer also uses the expression "Bloody Tragedy."
4. Daniel Horsmanden, *The New York Conspiracy, or a History of the Negro Plot* (New York: Printed and Published by Southwick and Pelsue, No. 3, New Street, 1810; reprinted in an abridged version with an introduction by Thomas J. Davis, Boston: The Beacon Press, 1971). This is the primary, and only contemporary, account of the trials, recorded by one of the three presiding judges. Other sources for these events include:

> Aptheker, Herbert. *American Negro Slave Revolts*. New York: Columbia University Press, 1943.
> Brawley, Benjamin Griffin. *A Social History of the American Negro: Being a history of the Negro Problem in the United States including a history and study of the Republic of Liberia*. New York: Macmillan, 1921, pp. 42–43.
> Coffin, Joshua. *An Account of Some of the Principal Slave Insurrections*. New York, 1860.

Greene, Lorenzo Johnston. *The Negro in Colonial New England*, with a preface by Benjamin Quarles New York: Atheneum, Columbia University Press, 1968.
Headley, Joel Tyler. *The Great Riots of New York, 1712–1837*. New York: Dover Publications, Inc., 1971.
McManus, Edgar J. *A History of Slavery in New York*. With a foreword by Richard B. Morris, Syracuse University Press, 1966.
————. *Black Bondage in the North*. Syracuse, New York: Syracuse University Press, 1973.
Miller, John Chester. *The First Frontier: Life in Colonial America*, New York: Delacorte Press, 1966.

5. Miller, *The First Frontier*, p. 159.
6. *The New England Weekly Journal* (Boston, Massachusetts: Printed by S. Kneeland and T. Green, printing house in Queenstreet), May 12, 1741, p. 1.
7. *The New York Weekly Journal*, June 22, 1741, page 3, column 2. Edgar J. McManus records that "in July a slave was hanged at Kingston, New York, for assault, an offense usually punished by flogging. In Roxbury, Massachusetts, a Negro suspected of stealing was seized and beaten to death by an enraged mob." (*Black Bondage in the North*, p. 139.)
8. Horsmanden, *The New York Conspiracy*, pp. 360–61.
9. Ola Elisabeth Winslow, *Jonathan Edwards 1703–1758: A Biography* (New York: The Macmillan Company, 1940), p. 87. Two sources for the Smith family of New York follow:

Smith, William, Jr. *The History of the Province of New York: From the First Discovery to the Year M.DCC.XXXII*. London: Printed for Thomas Wilcox, 1757. Reprinted and edited with an introduction by Michael Kammen, Cambridge, Massachusetts: The Belknap Press of Harvard University Press, 1972.
Upton, L. F. S. *The Loyal Whig: William Smith of New York and Quebec*. Toronto: The University of Toronto Press, 1969.

10. Horsmanden, *The New York Conspiracy*, p. 285.
11. "A Minister's Advice to Boston Slaveholders," in *The Negro Christianized: An Essay to Excite and Assist that Good Work, the Instruction of Negro-Servants in Christianity* (Boston 1706). Cotton Mather wanted black slaves to be able to read the Gospels. Boston slaveholders did not want black slaves to be able to read.
12. Greene, *The Negro in Colonial New England*, p. 161.
13. Horsmanden, *The New York Conspiracy*, p. 105. John Smith, also known as William Smith, was born in 1697 and was five years older than Jonathan Edwards. Smith graduated with an A.B. from Yale in 1719 and three years later took his A.M. From 1722 to 1724, he was a tutor at Yale

and at twenty-seven years of age he was offered the presidency of Yale. Smith turned to the law instead. After several years in England studying the law, he returned to New York and established a lucrative practice. He sided with the "Presbyterian faction" in 1727, entered politics, and defended John Peter Zenger in the famous freedom-of-the-press trial in 1735. After 1736, Smith dropped out of politics, turning to religious interests. He worked to gain a charter for a Presbyterian seminary in New Jersey. This College of New Jersey, the "Log College," later became Princeton University. John Smith also helped found the First Presbyterian Church in New York City and served as one of its elders. Smith probably met George Whitefield when the great itinerant stayed at Thomas Smith's house during his first visit to New York, in 1740. After the "Negro Plot" trials, Smith went on to become Attorney General of New York in 1751 and later served in the New York Supreme Court. He declined the chief justiceship. One of his fifteen children, William Smith, Jr., wrote the influential *History of the Province of New York*, published in London in 1757.

14. During the month before the July 8 Enfield sermon, eleven black slaves had been burned in New York and one in nearby Albany. At this time, Edwards was preparing for Enfield by delivering trial sermons. Ola Elisabeth Winslow (*Jonathan Edwards*, p. 191) notes:

> He had already preached three times from this same text. The first two sermons are undated; the third had been preached in Northampton immediately before the Enfield occasion. All three are distinctly different treatments of the same theme. In the first sermon, obviously early, he had presented the magnificence of God's wrath. It would be a glorious sight to see the world burn up in demonstation of such majestic power. The sermon ends with the contrasting picture of how it will be with those who are safe. . . . The third sermon, marked preached at Northampton, June, 1741, is essentially the same as the Enfield sermon. . . .

Topical sermons about the burning of black people at the stake would not be heard in the United States again until the lynch and torture epidemic reached its logical conclusion in the early decades of the present century.

15. All quotes from "Sinners in the Hands of an Angry God" in this chapter are from *The Works of President Edwards*, in eight volumes (Leeds: Printed by Edward Baines, 1811), 6:485–501.

16. John Calvin was trained professionally as a lawyer, and his theology dwells deeply on the law, obligation, and covenants. The legalistic elements in Calvinism were more prominent in Edwards's time than presently. Certainly the religious heritage influenced the noticeably litigious temperament of many New Englanders.

17. Edwin H. Cady, "The Artistry of Jonathan Edwards," The *New England Quarterly* (March 1949), pp. 61–72. See especially page 68.

18. Robert Lowell alludes to the fact that Pompey, the slave, was Jonathan Edward's birthday gift to his wife. Elisabeth D. Dodds suggests that the servant issue was of some concern in Edwards's life: "One reason Sarah [Edwards's wife] was able to cope smoothly with even such stylish guests was her extraordinary good fortune as an employer. Early on, a colored servant named Ruth came out from Boston to join the Edwards household. She stayed contentedly for many years. The diaries and letters of that era are full of complaints about how restless servants became away from the excitement of the cities. Other house-keepers on the frontier looked enviously at the durable Ruth (*Marriage to a Difficult Man: The "Uncommon Union" of Jonathan and Sarah Edwards*, [Philadelphia, Pennsylvania: The Westminster Press, 1971], p. 32). Slaves were seldom restless for "the excitement of the cities," so much as for the family and friends that they had been sold away from—unwillingly—in the first place. Mothers were frequently sold away from their children in New England. Dodds's claim that there was envy of the Edwards household in Northampton is significant. In the spring of 1741, the citizens of Northampton were "in great uneasiness" over the excessive standard of living in their pastor's household. The minister was thought to have "a craving disposition," and in later years he was "openly reproached in church meetings, as apparently regarding [his own] Temporal interest more than the Honour of Christ and the good of the Church" (Henry Bamford Parkes, *Jonathan Edwards: The Fiery Puritan* [New York: Minton, Balch and Company, 1930], p. 201. Parkes cited Edwards's letter after December 6, 1749, to his friend the Reverend Joseph Bellamy). In 1747, Edwards purchased the "Negro girl named Venus" for eighty pounds. One wonders if he sold her for a profit when he was dismissed from Northampton later and was forced to live more simply.
19. Winslow, *Jonathan Edwards*, p. 192. The cautious reader is advised that, beginning in the 1830s, with the rise of the abolitionist sentiment, thousands upon thousands of documents pertaining to the slave trade, including bills of sale and personal letters, were destroyed for fear that they would indicate that consumers benefiting from the slave trade in the North bore some responsibility for that trade.

4

Walter Elias Disney:
The Cartoon as Race Fantasy

*"And this also," said Marlow suddenly, "has been one
of the dark places on the earth."*

—Joseph Conrad
Heart of Darkness

The famous image of the Big Bad Wolf brings brilliantly to
life an entire range of Indian, black, and Jewish stereotypes.
In 1933, when "The Three Little Pigs" was released, millions
of misguided Americans were bewildered by the Depression
and blamed their troubles on the Negroes or on an alleged
international Jewish conspiracy. The specter of impending
racial rebellion again stalked the land. Playing on these fears,
the Big Bad Wolf quickly became the most popular cartoon
ever created. The Disney staff was dominated by animators
who, before traveling to California, had learned their trade
with Max Fleischer in Manhattan during the Harlem Renaissance of the Twenties. Fleischer's cartoons often featured the
voices and the talents of famous black performers, such as
Louis Armstrong, the Mills Brothers, and Cab Calloway of
the Cotton Club. Fleischer's cartoons referred directly to racial and sexual tensions. In sunny California, these concerns
were retained—but masked—by the slyly innocent charm that
later became the Disney trademark.

This ominous undercurrent in "The Three Little Pigs"
moved one *Literary Digest* writer to say, "Its theme song,

'Who's Afraid of the Big Bad Wolf?' had a haunting quality, which quite naturally brought it into pretty widespread fame and admiration."[1] Not only the song but the entire work is haunted. In exploiting the enormous success of the cartoon, the Disney staff released a hard-bound book version. Its cover illustration accurately reflects the fears of its creators: the Practical Pig is in the foreground, lecturing and warning his fellows on the need for hard work and preparation. The others are cheerfully indulging themselves in too much singing, dancing, and fiddling. All three are unaware of the Wolf in back of them—huge and hovering over all, drawn-out, and nebulous: a ghost. The haunted collective conscience of the Disney staff created in this cartoon an American *phantastikous*—a figure that serves "to make visible" the inner demons.[2]

In assaulting the brick house, the Wolf disguises himself as a Jewish peddler. He tips his stove-pipe hat and implores, "I'm the Fuller brush man, I'm working my way through collich." In the hard-bound book version, the phrasing is slightly different: "I'm de Fuller brosh man, I'm giving away free semples." Critic Richard Schickel has seen that

> Disney appears to have shared . . . the anti-Semitism that was common to his generation and place of origin. His studio was notably lacking in Jewish employees, and at least once he presented a fairly vicious caricature of the Jew on screen. . . . In the course of attempting to breach the solid defenses of the eldest pig's brick house, the wolf donned the robe, beard, and glasses of the long-caricatured Jewish peddler. It was an unfortunate choice for a gag. Despite the film's naiveté and its one glaring lapse of taste, one can still applaud "The Three Little Pigs."[3]

The Disney staff's racial fears of the Negro are depicted in more ways and with more finesse. The studio release immediately preceding "The Three Little Pigs" was "Mickey's

Mellerdrammer," in which the cartoon animals stage a happy version of Harriet Beecher Stowe's *Uncle Tom's Cabin*. The familiar Disney characters don the blackface. (Mickey gets his face comically blacked by accidentally exploding gunpowder.) Disney's Horace Horsecollar plays the whip-brandishing Simon Legree—"I *owns* ya—*body* and *soul!*" These cartoons were probably in production simultaneously in the early months of 1933. The issues, fears, and gags of "Mickey's Mellerdrammer" carried over into "The Three Little Pigs."

One gag is obviously the same in the two cartoons. At one point, Horace Horsecollar/Simon Legree crouches and pounds on a crate and whinnies; the wooden box rattles under the hooves. The Wolf assumes the identical posture in playing a trick on the three pigs. He fakes a retreat with "Well, they're too smart for me. Guess I'll go home!" and proceeds to crouch behind a stone wall, pounding on his knees to simulate fading footsteps. Both Simon Legree and the Wolf are stock villains: tall and lanky, long snouts and big teeth, shabbily dressed and mean, laughing harshly. Both are pelted with pies, apples, dead cats, and vegetables. The villain slave driver of "Mickey's Mellerdrammer" carried over into "The Three Little Pigs" via the Disney staff's overheated imaginations.

Walter Disney edited every story he produced. "The Three Little Pigs" was derived from three different versions of the British folktale. Precisely what attracted the man to these particular tales in the first place is a moot question, but what is important is the specific changes that he made in order to Americanize them. To make one seamless, psychologically satisfying whole, he had to select specific details and elements from the different versions. Disney's editing is instructive. What is left out is telling.

The names of the three pigs impressed the Disney staff: "The eldest of the three little pigs was called Browny, the second Whitey, and the youngest and best-looking Blacky."[4] These names are innocuous enough in England, but in Depression America, they were common and unpleasant. The Disney staff chose not to mention them—this would have made the mainsprings of their collective fantasy too obvious. The staff shared the common notion of those days that black skin was automatically somehow less clean than white. The Disney staff read a strange meaning into the British tale: Browny is "a very dirty little pig." Blacky is "a good, nice little pig, neither dirty nor greedy. He had nice dainty ways (for a pig), and his skin was always as smooth and shining as black satin."

The British tales describe the Wolf very sketchily. He will be sly and deceitful when he comes, the mother pig warns her brood. He will act friendly at first and will probably disguise himself. This is all. There is no physical description. Disney wanted to Americanize this vague figure. He sought a framework upon which to hang an apparition—a *phantastikous*—that would be frightening to both children and adults. He found his solution and his controlling metaphor in the stereotypes of the American Indian. Schickel comments:

> True, Disney was only an entrepreneur of low-level popular art, of family entertainment. But one catches a glimpse, an overtone, a perhaps unthinking hint of the American nightmare in all kinds of popular work no more elevated in its intentions than his—in the good westerns and in the adventures of the private eyes, in the surreal comedies of the Marx Brothers, in the vicious parodies of bourgeois longing that W. C. Fields used to make, surely in the wanderings of Chaplin's Tramp. How was it that Disney could never bring himself—or at least allow his employees—to allude to these great and constant themes of our culture? Why did he, by preference, huddle in the small town, or on the farm, forted up, as it were, against the wild beasts and the skulking Indians of the American imagination?[5]

If there was anything "unthinking" in Disney's actions, it was his willingness to exploit racial fears for profit, obliviously disregarding the human price in corruption. The critic's final question about "skulking Indians" provides its own answer. The Big Bad Wolf is visible proof of Disney's most formidable inner demon.

Described in the British tales as "slipping from tree to tree" when he appears, the Wolf became for Disney the American frontier settler's image of "an Indian behind every tree."[6] The Big Bad Wolf fits the "skulking" stereotype—sly, crafty, and shifty-eyed, with a slow, wary movement of the eyes from side to side. He makes repeated attempts to break into the houses or cabins by force or fraud. The innocent pigs are the settlers trapped in their isolated cabins during Indian "uprisings." Disney's hard-bound book version of "The Three Little Pigs" describes the Practical Pig's house as if it were on the frontier: "So the house must be doubly strong. It must be a fortress in which the little pigs must hide . . . " when the wolf is on the prowl for a meal and licking his chops. The almost ritual flight of the pigs from one house to the next during the cartoon is merely Disney remaining huddled up in the small town, "forted up, as it were."

Part of the "siege mentality" of the frontier settlers was an exaggerated fear of rape. There was the desire to defend the "purity of the race" and "the flower of white womanhood." The undercurrents of sex and violence in "The Three Little Pigs," masked by the Disney charm, were not lost on depression audiences.[7] The squealing and bouncing, pink and fat pigs are reminiscent of the protesting Victorian heroines of the melodramas Disney learned from: "No! No! A thousand times, NO! Not by the hair of my chinny chin-chin!" and the Wolf crying, "Let me in!" repeatedly. Struggling to get into one house, the Wolf loses his pants when the big button on his suspenders pops off. The green, patched pants fall down around his ankles, and the exasperated Wolf kicks them away. This incident makes sense only in the larger ethos of the frontier fears. In "The Three Little Pigs," as in much of Disney's work, there is a "derrière-assault propensity," as one critic described it. The temptation is ever to dismiss Disney for his obvious crudeness, in order to avoid facing his deeper and more disturbing implications.

The Big Bad Wolf is in all senses a great symbol for American violation. Guilty knowledge enforces its popularity, as critic Lewis Jacobs suggests:

> Today, when the real world is full of ruthless conflict, it is significant that Disney's films more than anyone else's (perhaps because he is the ablest of all) are full of ruthless conflict. Their violence, reaching extremes of destruction . . . finds its counterpart in the brutality of the modern world. . . . It is disturbing. . . . In an age in which might is so widely condoned, respected, and even glorified, the element of force is manifest in all contemporary mores. As the world popularity of his films proves, Disney is a most acute if unwitting interpreter of the violent spirit of the times.[8]

Under conditions in which gentleness and conscience are considered to be stupid, when the weak must be genuinely despised, there is no measure to despair. Apparently the American audiences laughed so hard partly from fear of recognizing complicity or of noticing the racial skeletons falling out of the closet.

In considering Disney's world, the black psychiatrist Frantz Fanon's words are worth extended quotation:

> If we want to answer correctly, we have to fall back on the idea of *collective catharsis*. In every society, in every collectivity, exists—must exist—a channel, an outlet through which the forces accumulated in the form of aggression can be released. This is the purpose of games in children's institutions, of psychodrama in group therapy, and, in a more general way, of illustrated magazines for children—each type of society, of course, requiring its own specific kind of catharsis. The Tarzan stories, the sagas of twelve-year-old explorers, the adventures of Mickey Mouse, and all those "comic books" serve actually as a release for collective aggression. The magazines are put together by white men for little white men.

This is the heart of the problem. In the Antilles—and there is every reason to think that the situation is the same in the other colonies—these same magazines are devoured by the local children. In the magazines the Wolf, the Devil, the Evil Spirit, the Bad Man, the Savage are always symbolized by Negroes or Indians; since there is always identification with the victor, the little Negro, quite as easily as the little white boy, becomes an explorer, an adventurer, a missionary "who faces the danger of being eaten by the wicked Negroes." I shall be told that this is hardly important; but only because those who say it have not given much thought to the role of such magazines. Here is what G. Legman thinks of them:

> With very rare exceptions, every American child who was six years old in 1938 had therefore assimilated at the very least 18,000 scenes of ferocious tortures and bloody violence. . . . Except the Boers, the Americans are the only modern nation that within living memory has completely driven the autochthonous population off the soil that it had occupied. America alone, then, could have had an uneasy national conscience to lull by creating the myth of the "Bad Injun," in order to be able to bring back the historic figure of the Noble Redskin vainly defending his lands against invaders armed with rifles and Bibles; the punishment that we deserve can be averted only by denying responsibility for the wrong and throwing the blame on the victim, by proving—at least to our own satisfaction—that by striking the first and only blow we were acting solely on the legitimate ground of defense. . . . There is still no answer to the question whether this maniacal fixation on violence and death is the substitute for a forbidden sexuality or whether it does not rather serve the purpose of channeling, along a line left open by sexual censorship, both the child's and the adult's desire for aggression against the

economic and social structure which, though with their entire consent, perverts them. In both cases the root of the perversion, whether it be of a sexual or of an economic character, is of the essence; that is why, as long as we remain incapable of attacking these fundamental repressions, every attack aimed at such simple escape devices as comic books will remain futile.[9]

"The Three Little Pigs," eight minutes long, made Walter Disney internationally famous. The Big Bad Wolf became so enormously popular, it seemed to demand an explanation by the cultural spokesmen. Even formal academics were surprised, and lauded "The Three Little Pigs" as a work of art—a rare blossom in the debased medium of the movies. A simple explanation was easily found: the Wolf was the threat of the depression, and the opposing Practical Pig was the durable American work ethic of thrift, clean living, and honesty. On the face of it, this explanation seems reasonable. As Raymond Durgnat commented, "Thirties comedy from 1929 until America began rearming in 1940, exists under the shadow of the Depression—a catastrophe represented, in so many political cartoons, inspired by Disney, as the big bad wolf huffing, puffing, and blowing down the houses of the three little pigs."[10] But the academic explanation is dull, dry, overly rational. It is what we expect to hear; it is basically evasive. Is it reasonable to reduce such a popular figure to the status of mere crude propaganda in favor of American conservative political thought?

This fantasy lives on with its sources unexamined and even unquestioned.[11] It is still strong enough to impress modern writers. The apt title of Edward Albee's *Who's Afraid of Virginia Woolf?* is a pun on the Disney title song, "Who's Afraid of the Big Bad Wolf?" Albee's play deals with the fears and fantasies that plague the members of a small, corrupted Connecticut academic community. The verbal duelling that is the hallmark of Albee's characters seems to be carried over from an earlier play, *The Death of Bessie Smith*."[12] As in "The

Three Little Pigs," there is the small group of characters—professors this time—forted up behind the walls of the Ivory Tower. All are quite powerless to prevent the damage that their self-imposed charades inflict upon them; the entire situation is complicated by sexual tensions. In alluding to Disney, Albee may be suggesting that the academics have been reduced to squabbling, backbiting stick figures in a one-dimensional cartoon existence. This is the comedy of blight.

Although produced by Disney, "The Three Little Pigs" was created by artists who had served their apprentice years with Max Fleischer during his heyday in the Twenties and had been deeply influenced by the uptown Harlem Renaissance. Fleischer's cartoons were informed by a more "liberal" attitude than Disney's. Fleischer presented racism and fear as evils, not "facts of life" and filled his cartoons with racial and sexual humor, addressing social tensions openly and directly. When his animators migrated to California with the depression, Fleischer lost ground as Disney's only serious competition. In California, Fleischer's animators retained all their social concerns, but, under the censorship of the Motion Pictures Production Code, learned to adapt to the charm and the cash in California.

The director of "The Three Little Pigs," Bert Gillett, left Fleischer for Disney in the spring of 1929. In the next year, he directed "Cannibal Capers" and "The Chain Gang." There were other Fleischer "refugees" as described by Bob Thomas:

> Ben Sharpsteen had worked for Max Fleischer on Happy Hooligan and Out of the Inkwell before coming to work for Walt in 1929. After the New York invasion began in full force, Sharpsteen grew discouraged over his ability to keep up with the new animators. Walt recognized Sharpsteen's capacity for working with young talent, and he suggested, "We've got to teach these new boys all about animation; you do it." Sharpsteen found himself in charge of training the fledgling artists, laying the

groundwork for an educational expansion in the mid-Thirties.[13]

Norman Ferguson arrived a few months later. In 1933, he was assigned the character of the Big Bad Wolf.

While "The Three Little Pigs" was in production, Max Fleischer released the six-minute cartoon "Snow White." This was a hallucinatory animated combination of the Grimm Brothers fairy tale and Harlem's Cotton Club bandleader, Cab Calloway, rendering his hit song, "St. James Infirmary Blues," in voice-over. The evil, white queen continually looks into her magic mirror and asks, "Am I the fairest in the place?" A black face continually answers her. A ghost sings the "St. James Infirmary Blues" in a darkened "mystery cave."

Isadore "Friz" Freleng came to Disney in 1927. After serving Walt Disney's California studios for years, he tried independent work. His "Clean Pastures"—a satire of playwright Marc Connelly's *The Green Pastures*—caricatured Louis Armstrong, Fats Waller, Cab Calloway, Bill "Bojangles" Robinson, Stepin Fetchit, and Al Jolson in blackface. Freleng's last musical cartoon was "The Three Little Bops," in which the original Disney cartoon is parodied in a story of three jazz musicians and a wolf whose trumpet playing is grievously white, or "straight."[14] He was just another man haunted by "The Three Little Pigs."

The great purpose of American popular art is to entertain and to alienate citizens from the reality, history, and concerns of other people—especially of exploited races. By peddling wish-fulfillment, common conceptions, and racial stereotypes, popular art serves to prevent the widespread appreciation of the wealth of our own historical experience. In the past century, a new mass public has emerged, willing to participate vicariously in a myth of success, at the cost of an inability to think critically and clearly or at all.

In a society that continually professes "self-reliance" and "individualism" to be sacred, but which is still riddled with primitive fears and demands the utmost conformity, leaders emerge who know how to exploit the pent-up sources of social creativity. Winston Churchill, in speaking of the potential new markets for movies in Asia and Africa, indicated his awareness that popular art may dominate and control the minds of men: "The English-speaking nations have here a great opportunity—and a great responsibility. The primitive mind thinks more easily in pictures than in words. The thing seen means more than the thing heard. The films which are shown amid the stillness of the African tropical night or under the skies of Asia may determine, in the long run, the fate of empires and of civilizations. They will promote, or destroy, the prestige by which the white man maintains his precarious supremacy amid the teeming multitudes of black and brown and yellow."[15]

"The Three Little Pigs" is a classic in American popular art, exploiting the public need to regard meaningful human strife as amusement. The popular notion that the Big Bad Wolf is the symbolic depression threat and the Practical Pig, a hard-work ethic or the conservative political philosophy of Herbert Hoover is simplistic and erring; but the underlying impulse to identify the cartoon with right-wing political propaganda is instinctively sound. The ennobling capacity of man to create symbols is strictly a two-edged sword.

The British novelist D. H. Lawrence, recording his impressions of the United States before going to Taos, New Mexico, in 1923, may as well have written the raison d'être for a certain cartoon:

> At present the demon of the place and the unappeased ghosts of the dead Indians act within the unconscious or under-conscious soul of the white American, causing the great American grouch, the Orestes-like frenzy of restlessness in the Yankee soul, the inner malaise which amounts almost to madness, sometimes. The Mexican is macabre and disintegrated in his own way. Up till now, the unexpressed spirit of America has worked covertly in the American, the white American soul. . . . When

you are actually *in* America, America hurts, because it has a powerful disintegrative influence upon the white psyche. It is full of grinning, unappeased aboriginal demons, too, ghosts, and it persecutes the white men like some Eumenides, until the white men give up their absolute whiteness. America is tense with latent violence and resistance. The very common sense of white Americans has a tinge of helplessness in it, and deep fear of what might be if they were not commonsensical.[16]

In all this, one is ever reminded that the first thing to do in placating the historical force of the "dead" past is to cease persecuting one's living neighbors.

Notes

1. "On the Screen," *Literary Digest*, October 14, 1933.
2. Walt Disney Studios, *Three Little Pigs* (New York: Jersey City Printing Co., 1933).
3. Richard Schickel, *The Disney Version: The Life, Times, Art, and Commerce of Walt Disney* (New York: Simon and Schuster, 1968), p. 95.
4. Katharine Mary Briggs, *A Dictionary of British Folk-Tales in the English Language* (Bloomington, Indiana: Indiana University Press, 1970).
5. Schickel, *The Disney Version*, p. 306.
6. This image remains popular: no explanation is necessary for the old depression joke: "Knock, knock." "Who's there?" "Formaldehyde," "Formaldehyde who?" "Formaldehyden places the Indians came running."
7. The spectacle of the Big Bad Wolf trying to seduce the three pigs from their secure fortress inspired the "Walls of Jericho" scene in the 1934 movie *It Happened One Night,* in which Clark Gable tells Claudette Colbert that "the walls of Jericho will protect you from the Big Bad Wolf!" as he hangs a dividing blanket in their single motel room.
8. *The Rise of the American Film; A Critical History, With an Essay: Experimental Cinema in America, 1921–1947* (New York: Teachers College Press, 1968), p. 499.
9. Frantz Fanon, *Black Skin, White Masks*. Charles Lam Markmann (New York: Grove Press, Inc., 1967), pp. 145–47. The author of *The Wretched of the Earth* here cites Gershon Legman's article, "Psychopathologie des Comics," French translation by H. Robillot, *Les Temps Modernes*, May 1949, pp. 919ff. Another author stressing the colonial aspects of Disney's

creations is Julian Halevy, an anthropologist who has worked with Indians in California and Mexico. In comparing "Disneyland and Las Vegas" (*The Nation*, June 7, 1958, pp. 510–13), Halevy relates the boat trip up the river in "Africa" in Adventureland to Joseph Conrad's journey in *Heart of Darkness*.

10. Raymond Durgnat, *The Crazy Mirror: Hollywood Comedy and the American Image* (New York: Horizon Press, 1969), p. 117.

11. Such is the case in the titling of Joan Mellon's book, *Big Bad Wolves: Male Sexuality in American Films*. The author fails to discuss Walter Disney.

12. Bessie Smith was a blues singer who died, some stories suggest, after having been refused admittance to a white hospital where treatment could have saved her life.

13. Bob Thomas, *Walt Disney: An American Original* (New York: Simon and Schuster, 1976), p. 112.

14. Leonard Maltin, *Of Mice and Magic: A History of American Animated Cartoons* (New York: McGraw-Hill Book Company, 1980), p. 269.

15. "Everybody's Language," *Collier's* (October 26, 1935), p. 24.

16. D. H. Lawrence, *Studies in Classic American Literature* (New York: The Viking Press reprint, 1964, original copyright 1923), pp. 36, 51.

5

Humphrey Bogart: The Slave Trader in Casablanca

Man's mind when tempered with time
Will return to the scene of the crime.
　　　　　　　　　　　　　—Homer

From the workmanlike practicality of the New England merchants who built their fortunes on the Atlantic slave trade, arose the romantic notion of "deepest, darkest Africa," where white heroes went to discover some terrific, redeeming truth that would set aright the moral compromises of their race. This theme is common to both Joseph Conrad's *Heart of Darkness* and Lee Falk's comic-strip *The Phantom;* "Imperialism, you see, is therapeutic. Trust Africa, that throbbing mystery, to exorcise the demons of the civilized soul."[1]

Arising in this tradition in 1942 is the popular movie *Casablanca,* in which the Humphrey Bogart character searches his soul in a dark place. The movie's evocation of Africa and its ancient trade is subtly pitched to the perfect degree. Without its allusions to the merchants of flesh, this fantasy would entirely lose its mystique. *Casablanca* is the perfect illustration of how close our most accepted images of integrity —including Rick Blaine as the honorable man of action—lie to our greatest failings. If Americans have successfully denied the voices and warnings of its own greatest writers, still they have not been able to avoid the silent *J'accuse* implicit in their popular art.

Casablanca was based on an original play titled *Everybody Goes to Rick's*, by Joan Alison and Murray Burnett, who remain virtually unknown. Burnett was a Cornell University graduate who met many of his interesting characters in a café in the south of France. James Agee once called this work "the worst play ever written," for reasons left unstated. The screenplay was by Howard Koch and the brothers Julius J. and Philip G. Epstein. The time is before Pearl Harbor. Rick Blaine (Humphrey Bogart) is the owner of the Café Américain in Casablanca. Sam (Dooley Wilson) is his piano player, fellow American, and only friend. Señor Ferrari runs the Blue Parrot, a rival café. Ferrari approaches Sam at his piano during working hours. In this first significant dialogue in the movie, the personal politesse matches the port's malaise:*

Señor.	Sam, how would you like to work for me at the Blue Parrot?
Sam.	Ah likes it fine with Mister Rick.
Señor.	I'll double whatever Rick pays you.
Sam.	But ah ain't got time to spend what ah makes here.

Rick's voice heard at this point. "My competition getting a little stiff for you, Señor Ferrari?" Sam gives a worried glance over his shoulder, but continues to play the piano. Señor Ferrari turns around very deliberately—not the least bit flustered by being discovered trying to lure Sam away. Then the scene includes Rick, who is smiling now, but not a pleasant smile.

Señor.	Hello, Rick.
Rick.	Hello, Ferrari. How's business at the Blue Parrot?
Señor.	Fine, but I'd like to buy your café.
Rick.	It's not for sale.

Señor.   You're doing very well, here, Rick. But
                then, I always like to see a man doing well.
Rick.   So out of your good will, you try to rob
                me of my piano player?
Señor.   "Rob" is a strong word.
Rick.   Is it?
Señor.   (thinking it over) Well, perhaps it
                isn't . . . but what I can't steal, I'm willing
                to pay for. What do you want for Sam?
Rick.   I don't buy or sell human beings.
Señor.   Too bad. That's Casablanca's leading com-
                modity. In refugees alone we could make
                a fortune if you would work with me
                through the black market.
Rick.   Suppose you let me run my business, and
                you run yours.[2]

Rick Blaine and Señor Ferrari are two white men in
Africa, discussing the stealing of the black man, Sam. The
"black market," aptly named, is a direct allusion to Casablanca's historical role as a way station on the slave-trading
routes. Arab middlemen conducted black slaves from the interior to the coast, where they were stored until an American
ship came with the right price. In *Casablanca*, "the black
market is a cluttered Arab street of bazaars, shops and stalls.
All kinds and races of people are milling about the merchandise which native dealers have on outdoor display. Both men
and women are dressed in tropical clothes. The canopies over
the stalls give them some protection from the scorching sun.
On the surface, the atmosphere is merely languid, but there
is the sinister undercurrent of illicit trade."[3]

In this first bit of dialogue, Humphrey Bogart delivers
the key line "I don't buy or sell human beings," while standing
at his bar, in a clipped, matter-of-fact, understated tone while
looking at the floor, crushing out a cigarette. For a man who
claims to have no ties with the black market, Rick Blaine's
real activity is problematical. The man is deceiving himself;
his policy of isolationism is a self-serving pose. The saloon-

keeper has other dealings with Señor Ferrari:

Señor. Good morning, Rick.
Rick.   I see the bus is in. I'll take my shipment with
        me.
Señor. No hurry. I shall have it sent over. Have a drink
        with me.
Rick.   I never drink in the morning. And every time
        you send my shipment over, it's a little short.
Señor. (chuckling) Carrying charges, my friend, carry-
        ing charges. (hailing a waiter) The bourbon.[4]

Behind this dialogue lies the African slave trade custom of
bartering in drink. French brandy was at first the most popular, until the Americans dominated the trade with their rum.
During bargaining sessions on the coast, the custom of "dash-
ing"—that is, tipping the various middlemen—soothed the
merchants' unruly dispositions. American traders became ad-
ept at getting the best bargain by getting their business com-
petitors to have one drink too many: "a dash too much."

The cynical Ferrari sees through Rick's pose of neutrality
with no difficulty. Since Rick Blaine seems to be such a sen-
sible, predictable merchant, Ferrari is baffled by the American's pose and is ironically amused. Even near the end of the
movie, Rick and the Señor are playing the white men haggling
over the dollar worth of the black man in the marketplace:

Señor. Oh—to get out of Casablanca—to go to Amer-
        ica—You are a lucky man.
Rick.   Oh, by the way—my agreement with Sam's al-
        ways been he gets twenty-five percent of the
        profits. That still goes.
Señor. I happen to know he gets ten percent. But he's
        worth it.[5]

When Rick decides to leave Casablanca, we never see him

talk about it with Sam. One of the magical things about the movie is this way in which Sam just disappears.[6] Where is Sam? In the larger ethos of *Casablanca*, the black man is "sold down the river." Audiences accept this because they sense that Rick Blaine is a latter-day slave trader, with Sam as his commodity.

"Cannot return to his own country—the reason is a little vague," Major Strasser, the Nazi officer, reads to Rick from his dossier, giving the saloon-keeper a questioning glance. Rick has done something in the United States that the authorities consider illegal—to the point of exiling him. The matter of Rick's crime is left open at the end of *Casablanca*. Audiences leave Humphrey Bogart's biggest movie never thinking to ask what this crime was. Since the entire first part of the movie is concerned with nothing but this, there is something more involved here. The British critic Barbara Deming observes that it is the dazzling Ilsa Lund (Ingrid Bergman) who totally distracts everyone:

> At the end of the film one thing remains altogether unexplained: why it was that he could never return to his country. For the purposes of the dream, this stray end is gathered up neatly enough with Ilsa's final departure. As Rick's eyes turn this last time to follow the plane's flight, the one exile is fused forever with the other; an audience is unlikely to remember that they are actually separate matters. For our purposes, though, the distinction stands and—to be altogether literal—does raise the whole question of a wider reference for the drama enacted than any love alone provides.[7]

It is possible to pinpoint the exact moment when this cinematic red herring goes into effect—when the crime story is masked by the love story. Ilsa Lund enters the Café Américain with Victor Laszlo (Paul Henreid), the Czech freedom fighter. Quickly, before Rick has seen her, Sam goes to Ilsa with the plea, "Leave him alone! Leave him alone, Miss

Ilsa!" but it is already too late. From the moment that Rick and Ilsa meet again, only the beautiful woman will represent Rick's past—not the black man. Rick will eventually clear up his romantic misunderstandings, but not his racial history. At the end, Rick has merely replaced his black friend Sam with the white Louis Renault (Claude Rains), the French prefect of police. Rick is going off to Free French Brazzaville—that is, deeper into Africa—instead of returning to the United States and a badly needed reconciliation with that country.

Casablanca is a "classic" because it raises the specter of the original crime committed by the United States against the world community, the slave trade, without dealing with it so clearly as to alienate the audiences fixed on pure entertainment. The movie is filled with oblique references to slavery, as if daring the American public to break through the blinding romantic mystique and figure it out. With cryptic dialogue, the screenwriters dimly hint at Rick's past. There is a critical dialogue between the saloon-keeper and Louis Renault, who makes a serious sport of trying to figure Rick out. Sharing a drink on the terrace of the Café Américain, the two men watch the takeoff, directly overhead, of the transport plane to Lisbon, and thence to the United States. Rick looks at it, "but his look isn't a happy one." Curiosity gets the better of Louis:

> Louis. You would like to be on it? I have often speculated on why you do not return to America. Did you abscond with the church funds? Did you run off with the President's wife? I should like to think you killed a man. It's the romantic in me.
> Rick. (sardonically) It was a combination of all three.

This is impenetrable and intended to be so.[8]

In headlong flight from a past that he finds too painful to acknowledge, Rick has forbidden Sam to play "As Time

Goes By," a song that says that one cannot run away forever because always "The fundamental things apply/ As time goes by."*[9] The reserved Rick does not react to anything emotionally until well into *Casablanca*, when he hears Sam playing this song. Furiously, he tells Sam, "I thought I told you never . . . ," but he is cut short by Sam's sidelong glance at Ilsa.

The most popular image of Humphrey Bogart is a still of Rick Blaine sitting at a table after hours in the Café Américain. Alone, darkened, brooding, sad, and self-pitying, proud, nursing a bourbon, he is the epitome of the haunted white man in Africa. He knows it will be a night for the heebie-jeebies.[10] The revolving searchlight from the airport periodically probes the darkened café, turning it into a prison or a haunted chamber to match its inmate. It reminds Rick of the flight to the United States that he will never take: "During the following scene the beacon continues its gyration, picking up first one speaker and then the other, in its sweep around the room." (The effect should be to create a mood of unreality that will make the flashback a plausible device.)[11]

Given the ethos of *Casablanca*, the dialogue between Sam and Rick is always pointed:

> Rick.   What time is it in New York?
> Sam.   My watch stopped.
> Rick.   I bet they're asleep in New York. I bet they're asleep all over America.[12]

Sam's watch has not stopped literally, but time, history, has stopped, so long as Rick so desperately resists facing any responsibility for the racial past. Time hangs heavily in the dialogue and imagery in *Casablanca*.

The romance of Rick and Ilsa may distract, but Sam is always there. At the Café La Belle Aurora in Montmartre,

*© 1931 (Renewed) Warner Bros. Music Inc.
    All Rights Reserved
    Used By Permission

Sam and Ilsa have a conversation—while Rick is out getting champagne—that indicates how deeply the screenwriters were concerned with race:

> Ilsa.   Sam—all the—how do you call them?—"hot" piano players say they never took a lesson in their lives. Of course, you never did, did you, Sam?
>
> Sam.   (gravely) Studied twelve years. Juilliard Foundation, New York.
>
> Ilsa.   (wryly) Well—all the best theories are going under these days.[13]

The "best theory" that goes under when Sam mentions Juilliard is the stereotype that all blacks have a "natural sense of rhythm." This natural sense is theoretically innate—that is to say, it is part of the "animal's" nature, which is perfectly and fully developed at birth. Music lessons would be merely superfluous, according to these notions, so common forty years ago. This "best theory" is convenient for those who also wish to believe that blacks have not sufficient intelligence to take music lessons. Sam tells Ilsa about the finest music school in the country because he does not wish to wear the mask for her. He speaks "gravely."

This conversation was completely eliminated from the final movie version. All that remains of it is the gesture that Ilsa makes towards Sam in pointedly including him in the champagne toast that they all make while gathered around the piano in Paris. The sight of a black man in a movie correcting a white woman in 1942 or of being on any such terms of familiarity would have deeply offended too many white audiences. *Casablanca* was liberal enough, in that regard, in showing Sam's friendship for Rick. Also, such a direct reference to the racial concerns of the screenwriters would have made the propaganda less effective. In *Casablanca*, all the sharp edges have been removed—except for the lancing irony in the dialogue. When Sam takes a glass of champagne from Rick, he says, "This sorta takes the sting outa being occupied, doesn't it, Mr. Rick?"

Moral corruption—more than the heat, hard work, disease and violence, and boredom—made drinking excessively one of the occupational hazards of the slave dealers. Accordingly, Rick Blaine is a character with a drinking problem. When Major Strasser asks him to state his nationality, Rick replies that he is a drunkard.

In *Casablanca,* drinking is a ritual and a moral act at times.

> Laszlo.   Won't you join us for a drink?
> Rick.   I'll join you. I never drink unless I'm alone.
> Renault. (with a laugh, as they sit) Well, that's a new turn on the old phrase—"Drink alone and like it."

Forty years ago, drinking alone was generally considered to be a sign of bad mental health. When Rick claims that he never drinks in the morning, he is probably not telling the whole truth. The saloon-keeper is ironic about his condition. He grimly fantasizes that Casablanca is a health spa. He jests that he has come to it for the waters.

Rick tells Ilsa during their first rendezvous in Casablanca that "I saved my first drink to have with you," but at the Arab's linen bazaar the next morning, he tells her, "I'm reasonably sober."

There is always a drink around Rick. The first time we see him, his hand is endorsing a bill, with a shot glass close by. While reassuring his customers that everything is all right, he almost without thinking sets up a wineglass that has been spilled. Later, drunk and blacking out, he knocks over his own bourbon—in the same manner in which Ilsa in Paris overturns her champagne. He also holds aloft a magnum and announces, "We have to drink this and three more . . . ," for the owner of the café would rather water his garden with his remaining wine than share it with the Gestapo. "Here, here, drink up! We'll never finish the other three!"

His bartender, Carl, says, "Monsieur Rick, you are getting to be your best customer," and Renault adds genially, "Well, Ricky, I'm very pleased with you. Now you're beginning to live like a Frenchman." In the hallway between the gambling room and the bar, Carl asks Rick solicitously, "May I get you a cup of coffee, M'sieur Rick?," but hears only a curt, "No, thanks." Rick offers the respectable young wife and Bulgarian refugee Annina Brandel a "Drink? Ah, of course not. Mind if I . . .?" Louis Renault jests that he must leave because as Chief of Police he would have to fine himself for drinking after the curfew. The movie's conversational small change almost always involves drinking: "Brandy?" or "We'll have a drink and go back to the hotel," or "We'll just forget about the drink."

The inmates of the Café Américain all seem to know about Rick's insistence on never drinking with his customers. When a table full of refugees asks Carl, the waiter, to invite Rick to join them, he informs them of this rule. Others need a little encouragement to remember it. Ugarte's offer of companionship is flatly rejected.

But there is the dramatic exception to this rule:

Laszlo.   Will you join us for a drink?
Renault. Oh, Rick never . . .
Rick.   Yes, I will.
Renault. Another precedent is being broken! Well, Ricky, you're becoming quite human!

Ilsa's presence mellows Rick Blaine—"Here's looking at you, kid"—but his memory of the Paris idyll is seen through the thick glass darkly: "We get the effect of the glass slowly turning into an hour-glass—the liquid flowing instead of sand."

The sources of the American romance with drinking lie in the clash between the Puritan conscience and the Yankee purchase of slaves with rum. In colonial New England, the slave trade *was* the liquor business. We deny this by pretending that the slavers were isolated, corrupt men working in Africa and by not acknowledging that the trade was a highly organized economic system built in the North. Starting in the late seventeenth century, the "trade in black ivory" grew to immense proportions. As fishing, farm, and forest products gave way before the slavers, who invested their profits in other activity, New England gained an edge in industrial competition. Profits went into textiles and the manufacture of spermaceti candles. Business soared high for sail lofts and ship chandlers' shops. Joiners, cabinetmakers, and silversmiths had all they could do to furnish the newly built houses of the slavers in New England, the mansions of Newport. Free enterprise was glorious; the price in human corruption would be paid by someone else.

Owners of slave ships were well-respected members of practically every New England community, even long after the trade was officially outlawed. Señor Ferrari boasts, "As leader of all illegal activities in Casablanca, I am an influential and respected man." Citizens derived a considerable sense of personal worth through their hard work and careers in the slave business. Large churches and their ministers wholeheartedly supported these ventures—their salaries were paid by generous contributions from the traders. When the prominent minister and scholar Ezra Stiles, president of Yale, needed household help, he bribed a coastal peddler with a barrel of rum to select a particularly fine "specimen" for him. It was the proper thing to do.

The fact that for centuries, Americans saw absolutely nothing unethical about stealing human beings bears mute testimony to the vast moral numbing suffered by all. Indignation was an emotion felt only when the price of flesh rose from one to fifty hogsheads of rum. It was no longer a "steal." Many a Puritan youth received his initiation into manhood, and his concept of culture, on the Guinea Coast: "One slaver from Upper Middletown (today Cromwell) on the Connecticut River was wrecked on the West African coast. Her master, James Riley, and his crew were captured by Arab traders, enslaved and taken across the Sahara Desert to Morocco."[15]

Fumigated slave ships would enter New England ports loaded with raw molasses from the West Indies, then called the Sugar Islands. The molasses was carted to distilleries near the wharves, to be manufactured into rum. There were twenty-two distilleries in Newport in 1761, sixty-three in and around Boston and Salem. Some of this rum, called O-Be-Joyful, was consumed locally. But most of it went to Africa in "rum vessels" to pay off the factors and middlemen who captured blacks and force-marched them to the coast. These middlemen often drank their profits and died by them: "It is incredible how many are consumed by this damnable liquor . . . which is not only confined to the soldiery, but some of the principal people are so bigoted to it, that I really believe for all the time I was upon the Coast, that at least one of their agents and factors innumerable died yearly of it."[16] How deeply Americans associate race, slavery, and drink is indicated even by the language. The word *bigoted*, which at first meant "addiction," now means race prejudice.

In the early nineteenth century, the burgeoning abolitionist movements planted a seed of doubt in the New England public's mind about the worthiness of the activity they were harboring. No longer was the pride of their manufacture called O-Be-Joyful. Many began to sense that alcohol was not to be the instrument of their economic salvation. The abolitionists saw drink as a hideous cultural weapon, the evil means used to deprive black people of their lives. The old stories were reconsidered, more credence given to the rumors that the rebels in the Jamaican slave revolt of 1760 had slit the Creole girls' throats, caught the bubbling blood in gourds, mixed it with rum, and drank it.[17] O-Be-Joyful was now "Demon Rum."

For colonials and the early temperance workers alike, the slave trade and the liquor business were the same thing. To speak out for abolition of slavery was to threaten the vested interests of the distilleries. Accordingly, abolitionists were often prohibitionists. Harriet Beecher Stowe, while visiting England, said, "The view of your great cities, flaming nightly with signs of 'Rum, brandy, and gin' is to the eyes of an American as appalling as the slave-market of our Southern States to an Englishman."[18] The famed abolitionists William Lloyd Garrison, Frederick Douglass, and Lyman Beecher attended the World's Temperance Convention in London.

> In 1828 Dr. Heman Humphrey, president of Amherst College, delivered a Fourth of July address which he called "A Parallel Between Intemperance and the Slave Trade." Slavery and not independence was his theme, he said, for "after the lapse of nearly fifty years of undisputed political freedom, the blood-freezing clank of a cruel bondage is still heard amid our loudest rejoicing"; and that bondage was the thralldom of intemperance. After a lurid description of the African slave trade and its infamous Middle Passage, Humphrey concluded with a still more unpleasant picture of the poverty, insanity, and other horrors attendant upon drunkenness.[19]

Idealistic southern advocates of temperance, with a little experience, came to see their noble cause as helping the abolition movement and abandoned both.

Antebellum churches found the temperance movement terribly contradictory. Most ministers agreed that sobriety was a virtue, but the official, conservative church policy was pro–liquor business. There were some comical, painful, and ambivalent moments:

> Even the Hard-shell Baptist church was not then ready to take a stand against whiskey. When Mentor Graham, the school-master, joined the temperance reform movement, the church trustees suspended him. Then, to hold a balance and hand out even justice all around, the trustees suspended another church member who had gone blind drunk. This action puzzled one member, who stood up and took from his pocket a quart bottle half full, which he shook till it bubbled, as he drawled: "Brethering, you

have turned one member out bec'se he would not drink, and another beca'se he got drunk, and now I wants to ask a question. How much of this 'ere critter does a man have to drink to remain in full fellership in this church?"[20]

Abraham Lincoln, a leading temperance reformer in Springfield, Illinois, gave an address on February 22, 1841, at the Second Presbyterian Church titled "Charity in Temperance Reform." Lincoln also felt slavery and drink to be closely associated: ". . . When there shall be neither a slave nor a drunkard on earth—how proud the title of that land which may truly claim to be the birthplace and the cradle of those revolutions that shall have ended in that victory. How nobly distinguished that people who shall have planted and nurtured to maturity both the political and moral freedom of their species."[21]

The violent emotions aroused by the idea of abolishing the slave trade were also aroused by the idea of curbing the rest of the trade: prohibition. This was a burning moral issue, fueled by racial guilts. When "Bleeding Kansas" voted to go "dry," the newspapers shouted, "The Saloon is as dead as Slavery!" And in the popular political song "Marching Through Georgia," the repeated refrain is, "Hurrah, hurrah, from rum we shall be free!"

The actual economic connection between liquor and the slave trade ended with the Civil War, but alcohol was still regarded as utterly evil—the agent of the Devil. If there was precious little charity in the temperance movement, it was for the simple reason that it was far easier to call Demon Rum the evil, rather than exorcise, or even acknowledge, one's own race hate. Later temperance reformers forgot the original connection of their movement with the slave trade and racial issues, but the violent passions continued. The malice and ugliness of the demagogue Carrie A. Nation's campaign of "hatchetation'" of saloons is bizarre, grotesque, and ludicrous, but perfectly comprehensible. She called herself "the John Brown of Prohibition." Worse excesses and hysterias over various drugs were to follow, all because "drug addiction is an emotion-packed issue. It touches on shadowy, vague areas of the human psyche. It stirs up ancient fears and releases vast reservoirs of hostility. At best, it is a most difficult question to deal with rationally. At worst, it encourages a lynch-mob mentality that feeds on itself. In one way or another, all of us are affected by what appears to be an unsolvable problem."[22]

Lillian Smith thinks that prohibition is incomprehensible when isolated from memories of "gullied fields and lynchings and Ku Klux Klan and segregation and sacred womanhood and revivals. . . ." She sees prohibition as the conservative heir of the liberal, nineteenth-century temperance movement, a form of right-wing politics used by whites to control their own racial hatreds:

> Especially must you be careful about what enters your body. Many things are prohibited. Among these, probably the easiest to talk about is alcohol. "Drinking" is a symbol of an evil that begins so early in life that it may be "inherited," for one who "drinks" moves almost from milk bottle to whiskey bottle, from the shaky legs of a child to the shaky legs of a drunk. The word *prohibition* means a movement to prohibit strong drink but everyone knows that stronger temptations are prohibited with it, just as one knows that *segregation* also shuts away from irresistible evils. Indeed, prohibition and segregation have much to do with each other, for there are the same mysterious reasons for both of these restrictions. . . .[23]

In short, one may be intemperate with many foreign substances that must be controlled: alcohol, marijuana, tea and coffee, the Negroes, the Russians. The great dream was that if these things were outlawed, they would also somehow magically cease to exist. It was a terrifying attitude: "What then is this universal, natural, and national remedy for intemperance? It is the banishment of ardent spirits from the list of lawful objects of commerce by a correct and efficient public sentiment, such as has turned slavery out of half of our land and will yet expel it from the world. . . . This, however, can not be done effectually so long as the traffic in ardent spirits is regarded as lawful, and is patronized by men of reputation and moral worth in the land. Like slavery, it must be regarded as sinful, impolitic, and dishonorable."[24]

The First World War, the Russian Revolution in 1917, and the failure of the United States troops to overthrow the Bolsheviks shortly after the war generated enough hysteria to create our national absurdity: Prohibition and the ugly repressiveness of the Volstead Act. Thomas Boylston Adams cites the wild words of a popular lecturer: "In America we are making the last stand of the great white race. If young America fails to conquer this destroyer alcohol, the human race will be doomed to go down from degeneracy to degeneracy till the Almighty in wrath wipes the accursed thing out." The affluent, sheltered white middle classes looked with horror on the "immigrant iniquity" festering in the saloons, the contemptible "café society," and reached for its legislative gun: "The Anti-Saloon League proclaimed, 'The Junker, the Kaiser are the merest incidents in bringing on this world holocaust. The all-compelling cause is a race of people who drink like swine. Their sodden habits have driven them towards brutality and cruelty. Beer will do for a nation exactly what it will do for an individual. We seek a saloonless and drunkless world.' "[25]

Humphrey Bogart plays Rick Blaine, the moral man in immoral society. He is, in his own estimation, a drunkard. When he tells Major Strasser this, Louis Renault comments that this makes him a "citizen of the world." Drinking is a moral act for this thirty-seven–year–old native of New York City. When the chief of police closes the Café Américain down for spurious reasons—except to collaborate with the Nazis—the audience in 1942 is on familiar Prohibition grounds. Humphrey Bogart is a "classic" in *Casablanca* because he portrays a man engaged by, but resisting, the offspring of Prohibition: gangsterism by government, by the people, under laws difficult to enforce and repulsive to obey.

Rick Blaine's fierce sardonicism is born of moral despair.
The apparent bankruptcy of democratic ideals has paralyzed
him:

Ilsa.   A franc for your thoughts!
Rick.   In America they bring only a penny—I guess
          that's all they're worth.

Rick always discourages anyone from going to America with
high hopes and bitterly exclaims, "All hail the happy days
when faith was something all in one piece." But Louis Renault
suspects that Rick's democratic liberalism is a corpse that
cannot be killed and warns not to try to help the Czech freedom fighter Victor Laszlo escape arrest by the Nazis:

Rick.   What makes you think I might do anything to
             help ?
Renault. I know your record. In 1935 you ran guns for
             Ethiopia, in 1936 you fought for Spain on the
             Loyalist side.
Rick.   (trying to make light of this) And got well paid
             for it on both occasions.
Renault. (pointedly) The winning side would have paid
             you more.
Rick.   (anxious for a change of subject) Maybe.[26]

On the face of it, Rick Blaine's career resembles that of
Victor Laszlo. It is not surprising that Rick fought for the
Loyalists in Spain with the International Brigade in 1936. But
running guns for Ethiopia in 1935—the white man smuggling
guns for blacks against Italian Fascists—is a standout. Rick
gets very nervous when this past is mentioned and not only
because it is politic not to appear to be too good. He cannot
bring himself to say openly that the democratic ideals that he
struggled for once are worthy ones. Rick claims that money
was his motive—not only to avoid being backed into a corner
too easily, but also to express his contempt for the unfettered
confidence of Laszlo: "He's the last man I want to see in

America." But it is the irrevocable moral compromise of Rick's crime and exile that has reduced him to a suicidal despair. He asks Ilsa to do him the favor of shooting him.[27]

Across the map of Africa at the beginning of *Casablanca* is traced the route taken by the refugees fleeing from Europe to Casablanca. There is documentary footage depicting homeless people traveling by every available means. Casablanca was the bottleneck to release, not only from political extremes, but also from vultures like Ugarte, who has murdered two German couriers, stealing the two priceless "letters of transit, signed by Charles deGaulle—cannot be rescinded." The basic situation in the movie—two exit visas for three people, with one person to be forced to give up his chance so that another might escape certain death—was a familiar reality in 1942. In the face of the strict immigration quotas, thousands turned in despair to friends and relatives, seeking any way out of the trap. Refugees stood outside every American consulate through the night, waiting to register their names.

Audiences watching *Casablanca* in 1942 knew that they were getting the official government line on United States immigration policy, especially regarding European Jews. During the decade leading up to World War Two, Adolf Hitler taunted the U.S. State Department for its refusal to relax its strict immigration quotas. Hitler turned American apathy into a weapon for himself. In his own manner in 1933, he announced that American citizens had no right to protest his anti-Semitism, because the United States itself practiced racial discrimination in its immigration policies. His words were widely reported: "Through its immigration law, America has inhibited the unwelcome influx of such races as it has been unable to tolerate in its midst. Nor is America now ready to open its doors to Jews fleeing from Germany. . . . We merely wish to state that the United States posseses rigorous immigration laws while Germany has absolutely none thus far. We further point to American relations with Negroes—social and political. And finally, certain American universities have long since excluded Jews. . . . We are saying openly that we do not want the Jews while the democracies keep on claiming that they are willing to receive them—and then leave the guests out in the cold! Aren't we savages better men after all?"[28]

When the United States rejected the fleeing passengers on the SS *St. Louis* after their last-minute escape from Germany, Hitler had long since known that he could do anything to the Jews and not fear anything from the American government. The fact of the matter was—beyond Hitler's half-truths—that the intransigence of the State Department in sticking to the letter of the immigration law did have an anti-Jewish element. This intransigence was compounded of diplomatic evasion, attitudes of isolationism, indifference, raw bigotry, and political expediency—noticeably Franklin Roosevelt's knuckling under to pressure from American "patriotic" groups:

> In the United States, John B. Trevor and his patriotic confederates opposed every move to liberalize immigration. Trevor also headed a Committee on Immigration and the Alien Insane under the unlikely auspices of the New York Chamber of Commerce. In May 1934 a report prepared for that committee was mailed to all chamber members. Its recommendations included: no exceptional admission for Jews who are refugees from persecution in Germany; no admission for any immigrant "unless he has a definite country to which he may be deported, if the occasion demands"; and no admission to immigrants whose ancestors were not "all members of the white or Caucasian race."[29]

> The "patriotic" and restrictionist groups did not wait long to assert their views about the admission of two hundred and fifty Jewish children. The American Coalition of Patriotic, Civic and Fraternal Societies, led by Captain John B. Trevor and numbering such stalwarts as the Sons and Daughters of the American Revolution, Veterans of

Foreign Wars and the American Legion Auxiliary, registered immediate objections. According to the Coalition, the State and Labor departments were allowing "international sentimentality" to run riot.[30]

Expressions like "international sentimentality," "sobbing sentimentalists," "crybaby personalities," and "bleeding hearts," to describe anyone professing humanitarian values are sneers of hatred and contempt that, along with "café society types," are also code words for the popular expression "nigger-lover." As a movie that tried to oppose the values of Hitler and company, *Casablanca* takes a stand against such "patriotism." The word *sentimentalist* is mentioned frequently. Louis says to Rick, "I suspect that under that cynical shell, you're a sentimentalist at heart. . . ." When Rick later lets the refugee Annina's husband, Jan Brandel, win at roulette on the fixed wheel—thus giving him the money needed to bribe Louis—Louis expresses his disappointment with Rick: "As I suspected—you're a rank sentimentalist." But near the end of the movie, this initial contempt has become "Well, Ricky, I was right. You're not only a sentimentalist, but you've become a patriot." There is admiration in Louis' voice.

Casablanca is a deliberated work of propaganda in favor of Washington policies. It was carefully released to New York audiences at the Hollywood Theater on Thanksgiving Day, 1942—eighteen days after the Allied landing of November 8 on the coast of French North Africa, at Oran, Algiers, and Casablanca. The general release on January 23, 1943, came in the middle of the conference between Roosevelt and Churchill at Casablanca. The United States government, ever mindful that half the population before Pearl Harbor was pacifist and isolationist, approved of the idea of making Rick Blaine's disillusionment a symbol for those attitudes of pacifism and isolationism, which it thought should be discarded immediately. The movie could be released only because the neutral Rick Blaine eventually commits himself to the Allied cause—at least, to all appearances. The agents for this propaganda were the screenwriters Julius and Philip Epstein, who wired their script revisions to Howard Koch at the studio from Washington, where they were working on Frank Capra's series of domestic propaganda shorts, *Why We Fight*.

In this self-consciously internationally cast drama, characters represent not only individuals, but their countries and ideologies as well. Germany, Free France, the Vichy regime, the Soviet Union, Czechoslovakia, Sweden, Bulgaria, and the United States are all represented. Alone among these nations, the United States is given two characters, one black and one white, as if to prove democracy in action—as in all those carefully integrated platoons invented by wartime Hollywood, or as in the movie *Lifeboat*, wherein each survivor of the shipwreck tells his own particular story—except for the black man, who is left out. In fact, the best part is left out of *Casablanca:* "It's never mentioned in the film that neither the Germans nor the French have any business having their armies in Morocco. The French are as culpable for ruling Casablanca as the Germans are for ruling Paris, yet nowhere in the film is there a hint of this contradiction. Apart from being corrupt, Captain Renault's power in Casablanca is not shown as socially unjust. Ostensibly those singing the 'Marseillaise' are making a gesture against tyranny but it is hard to imagine the singing of a patriotic Moroccan song bringing the same reaction."[31] Once again, American popular art succeeds in blinding an unheeding public to world realities. The movie's terrible message is that personal, individual happiness must be sacrificed, in order that the world may yet be saved for democracy—and for the profits from our colonization of darker races.

What is strictly forbidden is reconciliation. The exile must be kept running away from himself, forever condemned to his own integrity:

    Rick.   Ilsa, I'm no good at being noble. But it doesn't take much to see that the problems of three little people don't amount to a hill of beans in this crazy world. Some day you'll understand that.

127

Rick convinces Ilsa to get on the plane, ultimately, because he knows that the illegal trade is not something a lady can be any part of. Victor Laszlo, the man of absolute faith, says proudly, "Now I *know* our side will win!"—assuming that Rick intends to join the cause. Rick remains silent, not taking the trouble to disillusion the freedom fighter. Nothing has changed for him: there is a terrible fatality in his final glance at the departing plane overhead. Rick is free only to wander deeper into Africa, to more drinking, more compromise.

It is as this exile that Humphrey Bogart haunts us. He saunters from a bank of fog, encased in the trench coat, his collar raised, the shoulders hunched, his face half concealed by the hat brim. He drags on a cigarette, slowly and thoughtfully. Then the street lamp illuminates only the place where he once stood. Like the homeless in Casablanca, he seeks an honest place. Rick Blaine must "wait . . . and wait . . . and wait."

Notes

1. Mac Margolis, "The Pen and the Pith Helmet," The *Boston Phoenix*, January 6, 1981, section 3, pp. 1, 14.
2. John Gassner and Dudley Nichols (eds.), *Best Film Plays of 1943–1944* (New York: Crown Publishers, 1945), p. 641.
3. Howard Koch, *Casablanca: Script and Legend* (Woodstock, New York: The Overlook Press, 1973), p. 110.
4. Gassner and Nichols, *Best Film Plays*, pp. 665–66. Rick Blaine does not drink with the black marketeer because that would mean admitting, through the drinking ritual, that he is involved. Men deeply implicated in the African trade frequently denied any complicity whatever. The exchanges between Rick and Señor Ferrari bear an uncanny resemblance to this conversation between an Englishman, Richard Jobson, and one Buckor Sano in 1623: "Further upriver, the African trader with whom he was doing business, his friend Buckor Sano, showed him a group of young Negresses standing together, and told him they were slaves for him to buy. 'I made answer,' writes Jobson, 'we were a people who did not deal in any such commodities, neither did we buy or sell one another, or any that had our own shapes; he seemed to marvel much at it, and told me it was the only merchandise they carried down into the country." (James Pope-Hennessy, *Sins of the*

128

Fathers; A Study of the Atlantic Slave Traders (1441–1807) [New York: Capricorn Books, 1969], p. 45

5. Gassner and Nichols, *Best Film Plays*, p. 688.

6. Sam's abrupt dismissal is more significant, as these two Americans "represent" the United States in this self-consciously internationally cast movie.

7. Barbara Deming, *Running Away from Myself: A Dream Portrait of America Drawn from Films of the Forties* (New York: Grossman, 1969), chapter 2.

8. Louis Renault suggests, with the phrase "abscond with the church funds," a moral crime and theft; with "run off with the President's wife," a crime national in scope, involving breaking up a family and rape; and murder. These were all routine aspects of the New England merchants' activities on the coast.

9. Sam is like a Greek chorus—the whispering, pianissimo voice of conscience. "As Time Goes By" recollects "hearts filled with passion, jealousy, and hate." The song "S-H-I-N-E" mentions " 'Cause my hair is curly/ 'cause my teeth are pearly."* When Rick slips the stolen letters of transit into the piano for hiding, it's "Who's Got Trouble?" When Ilsa enters the café, it's "Love For Sale." When the Vichy police raid the place, Sam leads a group sing of "Old Noah, What Did He Do?" ("He built himself a floating zoo," as the camera pan picks up "all types of people.") And as for the rendition Dooley Wilson gives for "It Had To Be You"—interpreting words as if they were spoken by a slave to his white master—mere words cannot express the depth of the irony:

> I wandered around, finally found
> Somebody who could make me be true,
> Could make me feel blue,
> Even be glad, just to be sad,
> Thinking of you.

> Some others I've seen
> Might never be mean,
> Might never be cross
> Or try to be boss,
> But they wouldn't do.

*Copyright MCMXLVIII Shapiro, Bernstein & Co. Inc. Renewed. Used by permission.

> Nobody else gives me a thrill.
> With all your faults,
> I love you still.
> It had to be you, wonderful you.
> It had to be you.*

10. Billy De Beck coined the expression that meant "the jitters" with his popular song from 1926 "Heebie-Jeebies."

11. Gassner and Nichols, *Best Film Plays*, p. 655.

12. This is another stab at "isolationism," the screenwriters' political stalking horse.

13. Gassner and Nichols, *Best Film Plays*, p. 658.

14. The slave trade was regarded by many—especially its victims—as a form of "occupation." Sam continues his accustomed ironic banter at his white man in Africa. Although Sam is on terms of greater equality with Rick than most black characters with white ones in other films of 1942, still he is, as noted by Harvey R. Greenberg, "a slightly liberalized version of that old Hollywood favorite, the faithful family retainer of the ante-bellum plantation house" (*Movies on Your Mind: Film Classics on the Couch from Fellini to Frankenstein* [New York: Saturday Review Press, E. P. Dutton and Co., Inc., 1975], p. 91). The comically "popped" and rolling eyes of Sam are also a concession to the expectations of the complacently condescending white audiences.

15. Clifford Lindsey Alderman, *Rum, Slaves and Molasses; The Story of New England's Triangular Trade* (Folkstone, England: Bailey Brothers and Swinfen, Ltd., 1972), p. 110. The slave trade was euphoniously and geometrically called the "Triangular Trade" because of the geographical configuration of Africa, the West Indies, and the United States.

16. Pope-Hennessy, *Sins of the Fathers*, p. 160.

17. Ibid., p. 143.

18. Edward Wagenknecht, *Harriet Beecher Stowe: The Known and the Unknown* (New York: Oxford University Press, 1965), p. 192.

19. Alice Felt Tyler, *Freedom's Ferment* (Minneapolis, Minnesota: The University of Minnesota Press, 1944), p. 324.

20. Carl Sandburg, *Abraham Lincoln: The Prairie Years* (New York: Harcourt, Brace, and Co., 1936), pp. 165–66.

21. Ibid., p. 275.

22. John Rublowsky, *The Stoned Age: A History of Drugs in America* (New York: Putnam, 1974), p. 199. Antiabortion is a late symptom.

23. Lillian Smith, *Killers of the Dream* (New York: W. W. Norton and Company, Inc., 1949), pp. 87–88.

24. Tyler, *Freedom's Ferment*, p. 323.
25. Thomas Boylston Adams, "History Looks Ahead," the *Boston Globe* column.
26. Neither Rick's political disillusionment expressed here nor his evasiveness is explained by the romance with Ilsa.
27. In running guns to Ethiopia, Rick Blaine is a smuggler. This echoes the historical development beginning in 1808 with the outlawing of the slave trade: the merchants became professional smugglers. Throughout his entire movie career, Humphrey Bogart played characters who bootlegged alcohol, ran rum and guns and political refugees, as in *To Have and Have Not*, and liquor was found even in the presence of that strange missionary woman in *The African Queen*. There is a scene in *The African Queen* where many empty gin bottles float all in a row down the Ulanga River.
28. Arthur D. Morse, *While Six Million Died; A Chronicle of American Apathy* (New York: Random House, 1975), pp. 145, 146, 288.
29. Ibid., p. 166.
30. Ibid., p. 165.
31. Koch, *Casablanca*, p. 223. These are the words of a Stanford University graduate, Walter Bougere.

6

Ritual in American Childhood

—William Butler Yeats
"Among School Children"

The near approach of the wild and the senseless frightens sometimes to the point of paralysis. In dignified panic, man resorts to ceremony and ritual, "in order to overcome . . . fear and horror by giving it a form and an image. . . . One of the characteristics which seems to distinguish man from all other animals is this desire to impose a pattern on what mystifies and frightens him."[1] Franz Kafka has a parable about such ritual: "Leopards break into the temple and drink to the dregs what is in the sacrificial pitchers; this is repeated over and over again; finally it can be calculated in advance, and it becomes part of the ceremony."[2] If suffering is beyond meaning, we light an "imbecile candle in the heart of that almighty forlornness." Ritual enables us to endure catastrophe without paralysis. Lord Raglan observed that "the essential truth of

*Reprinted with permission of Macmillan Publishing Company from THE POEMS OF W. B. YEATS edited by Richard J. Finneran. Copyright © 1928 by Macmillan Publishing Company

the myth lies in the fact that it embodies a situation of profound emotional significance, a situation, moreover, which is in its nature recurrent, and which calls for the repetition of the ritual which deals with the situation and satisfies the need evoked by it."[3]

We placate our national demons at the price of committing social, political, and moral excesses. Catastrophe may be happily forgotten, but "when 'advanced' societies insist on maintaining the fiction that they engage in no harmful acts . . . they act like 'benevolent' individuals who insist on maintaining the fiction that they engage in no harmful acts. . . ."[4] Ritual gives us the answers that we want: "Mirror, mirror, on the wall, who's the fairest of them all?" In "The Imagination of Disaster," Susan Sontag sees that our ceremonies can be in the cinema: our "largely debased" popular art enables us to continue to

> . . . live under continual threat of two equally fearful, but seemingly opposed, destinies: unremitting banality and inconceivable terror. It is fantasy, served out in large rations by the popular arts, which allows most people to cope with these twin spectors. For one job that fantasy can do is to lift us out of the unbearably humdrum and to distract us from terrors—real or anticipated—by an escape into exotic, dangerous situations which have last-minute happy endings. But another of the things that fantasy can do is to normalize what is psychologically unbearable, thereby inuring us to it. In one case, fantasy beautifies the world. In the other, it neutralizes it.[5]

Popular American art is the temple wherein the ceremonial icons are worshipped. The icons and the images seem to be *sui generis* to the devout—self-born, pure. Uncorrupted by love or history, these images command awe and adoration. The sacred origins are never questioned by the pious. But the price of keeping icons is steep, and inevitably the difficulty that initially precipitated the ritual will erupt amid personal dissolution:

Those masterful images because complete
Grew in pure mind, but out of what began?
A mound of refuse or the sweepings of a street,
Old kettles, old bottles, and a broken can,
Old iron, old bones, old rags, that raving slut
Who keeps the till. Now that my ladder's gone,
I must lie down where all the ladders start,
In the foul rag-and-bone shop of the heart.*[6]

So long as men die, ritual will be passed on to the young. The chants and the incantations endure in children's games. In "rational," educated society, given to bogus intellectual conceits and pretensions, the truly primitive is relegated to the cultural scrap heap of childrens' activities—mere relics of their former grandeur: "It is among the youngest in a community that tradition remains longest unspoiled, for children are great mimics; they possess highly imaginative and inventive energies, they are intensely dramatic, but above all, they are dyed-in-the-wool conservatives."[7] The child who tries to change the rules of the game is quickly corrected by his or her peers. Radical change offends the child's natural sense of "fair play."

In medieval society, children were introduced directly to the adult world. The extended "childhood"—a recent invention of the newly arisen and sheltered middle classes—artificially "separates" children from adult concerns. But the rituals of children remain unnervingly close to adult manners:

> Lizzie Borden took an axe
> Gave her mother forty whacks.
> When she saw what she had done
> She gave her father forty-one.

It is not recorded how the children of Fall River, Massachu-

*Reprinted with permission of Macmillan Publishing Company from THE POEMS OF W. B. YEATS edited by Richard J. Finneran. Copyright © 1940 by Georgie Yeats, renewed 1968 by Bertha Georgie Yeats, Michael Butler Yeats and Anne Yeats

setts, in 1892 came to sing this little song. Like any ritual, there is present a genuinely haunting element. Since children—and criminals—have no articulated concept of guilt, it is particularly unnerving to see in this refrain an indication that guilt—"when she saw what she had done"—plays a part in increasing her fury: "she gave her father forty-one." Elizabeth Borden, found "not guilty" by a Victorian male jury because respectable women simply did not do such things, was condemned literally out of court by the children. Yet it is preposterous to claim that children knowingly judge adults. There is a mystery in the ritual. What seems to predominate among the children as well as with adults is the effort to deal with terror.

Of deeper social import is the most popular counting-out rhyme in the United States, at least until the late 1950s:

> Eeny, meeny miny, mo
> Catch a nigger by the toe,
> If he hollers let him go,
> Eeny, meeny miny, mo.[8]

The first line is of ancient British origin:

> The inhabitants of the British Isles just two thousand years ago—at the time of the Roman conquests—were people of the Iron Age phase of culture. They painted their bodies with woad, believed that babies born with one or two teeth were vampires or at least fearsome creatures, held that divination of the future could be attained through magic rhymes—and celebrated a blood-thirsty ritual in which human sacrifices were made by burning people in wicker cages. There seems to be some evidence, for instance, that *eeny, meeny, miny, mo*—which almost certainly goes back to the Druids—was originally a divination rhyme or else a system for selecting the victim for human sacrifice. In short, the ancestors of today's English gentlemen were living in a state not far removed from that of many nonliterate peoples when the

Romans appeared on the scene and began taking the captured aborigines back to Italy for the slave market, and the word got around that they were not a very good buy. Too primitive.[9]

Only in America did the British "Catch a chicken by his toe"—or a tinker, or a rooster—become "Catch a nigger by the toe." The word nigger is common in American folklore but is unknown in any English traditional rhyme or proverb. Charles Francis Potter (*Harper's Bazaar*, May, 1950) compares the rhyme with the French-Canadian game "Meeny, meeny, miney, mo Cache ton poing derriere ton dos. . . ." and suggests that the "Catch a nigger by his toe" line is an American corruption of it about 100 years ago.[10]

The counting-out rhyme used to choose the leader for the games requiring a central player is believed to have come from the magical signs and incantations of the dim past and is generally accepted as a just and impartial method of selecting the leader. He is called "it."

The player that counts out—that is, the one who chooses the leader—is the player that first shouts "Count Out." He is accepted by the group, who then stand about him as he recites lines of doggerel, alloting one word to each player by pointing to him as he speaks. The rhyme is repeated till the last word spoken eliminates the player spoken to. Finally, only one player remains, and he is "it."[11]

The lines native to New England, "Catch a nigger by the toe/ If he hollers let him go," are clearly a response by children to the adult slave trade. Children learn early that one had to "catch a nigger," often by the ankles with chains, in Africa. The slavers' preference for blacks who did not protest too much or too long is reflected in the advice "If he hollers, let him go." An American variation states, "If he hollers make him pay/Fifty dollars every day. O-U-T spells out, and out goes she, in the middle of the deep blue sea."[12] It was well known that diseased or incorrigibly rebellious slaves on the

Middle Passage to the Sugar Islands would be cast into "the middle of the deep blue sea." Scores of slaves could be chained to the anchor cable and cast overboard in order to avoid detection after 1808, when the slave trade was made illegal in the United States. In yet another variation, there is the memory of the auction block: "If he hollers, let him go/ My mother says to choose the very best one." Since every socially prominent family owned slaves, mothers usually were employers interested in getting "the very best one." Children used to crowd the docks when the slavers came in, to taste the molasses. The ships' cargo holds still smelled from the Middle Passage. The counting-out ritual served—as ritual must—to keep terror at bay.

> London Bridge is falling down,
> Falling down, falling down,
> London Bridge is falling down,
> My fair lady.

In pagan and medieval Europe and England, it was believed that the soul, at death, separated from the body and was forced to cross a bridge before reaching its final resting place. In Sweden's Täby District, near Stockholm, about twenty rune stones over 1,000 years old, placed along a roadside, honor a local man of achievement, one Jarlabanke. One stone near a causeway reads: "Jarlabanke had three stones raised in memory of himself while he still lived. And he built this bridge for his soul. And alone he owned the whole of Täby. God help his soul."

Sanctity was therefore attributed to the builders of bridges, for the Devil, in league with the local river god, opposed bridges as invasions of their domain.[13] It was well known that bridges were always falling down. Ancient people knew that their engineers and masons faced supernatural opposition. In "London Bridge," the religious edifice must be continually rebuilt:

> Build it up with wood and clay

> Wood and clay will wash away
> Build it up with bricks and mortar
> Bricks and mortar will not stay
> Build it up with iron and steel
> Iron and steel will bend and bow
> Build it up with silver and gold
> Silver and gold will be stolen away.[14]

The last four lines here are fairly modern additions, indicating an awareness of physical and human reasons for falling bridges that are not present in older versions.

Since it is felt that the bridge cannot be made to stand by ordinary human strength, a "watchman" is set to overcome the malicious forces of nature:

> Then we must set a man to watch
> Suppose the man should fall asleep?
> Then we must put a pipe in his mouth
> Suppose the pipe should fall and break?
> Then we must set a dog to watch
> Suppose the dog should run away?
> Then we must chain him to a post.[15]

The "watchman" who sleeps in London Bridge represents the man, woman, or child who was ritually killed in pagan times as a human sacrifice to placate the deities, which might otherwise be hostile, in what have come to be called foundation rites.

> It is known that great erections entailed human sacrifice; but there was no particular code of ethics as to how the sacrifice should be secured. The unwary traveler peacefully going about his own affairs was quite likely to be seized and beheaded for these rites. That would appease a horrid deity.

Of the building of the Tower of London in the twelfth century, Fitzstephen writes that the mortar was mixed with the blood of wild beasts. And it is said the secret of the ancient Irish masons' fine craft was this very mixture of blood and sand. It is well known that men's heads often decorated the bridges and gates of a city, and it is reasonably conjectured that there was other blood in the masonry than that of beasts.[16]

Iona and Peter Opie describe these widespread rituals:

In Germany as recently as 1843, when a new bridge was to be built at Halle, the notion was abroad among the people that a child was wanted to be built into the foundation. When the Bridge Gate at Remen was demolished in the last century, the skeleton of a child was found embedded in the foundations. The bridge of Aryte in Greece is said to have kept falling down until they walled in the wife of the master-mason. The building of the bridge of Rosporden in Brittany is another case where legend has it that all attempts were unsuccessful until a four-year-old boy was immured at the foot of it. Further, the legend goes, the little boy was buried with a candle in one hand and a piece of bread in the other. Food and light was given so that the guardian might keep alive and watchful, which immediately recalls the words of the old Stuart lady:

Suppose the man should fall asleep?
Then we must put a pipe in his mouth.

. . . And London Bridge itself is not without a tainted reputation, for there is in the capital a tradition that the stones of this great bridge, too, were once bespattered with the blood of little children.[17]

Sir James G. Frazer knew the persistence of human ritual:

In modern Greece, when the foundation of a new building is being laid, it is the custom to kill a cock, a ram, or a lamb, and to let its blood flow on the foundation stone, under which the animal is afterwards buried. The object of the sacrifice is to give strength and stability to the building. But sometimes, instead of killing an animal, the builder entices a man to the foundation stone, secretly measures his body, or a part of it, or his shadow, and buries the measure under the foundation stone; or he lays the foundation stone upon the man's shadow. It is believed that the man will die within the year. The Bulgarians still observe a similar custom. If they cannot get a human shadow they measure the shadow of the first animal that comes that way. The Roumanians of Transylvania think that he whose shadow is thus immured will die within forty days; so persons passing by a building which is in course of erection may hear a warning cry, "Beware lest they take thy shadow!" Not long ago there were still shadow-traders whose business it was to provide architects with the shadows necessary for securing their walls. In these cases the measure of the shadow is looked on as equivalent to the shadow itself, and to bury it is to bury the life or soul of the man, who, deprived of it, must die. Thus the custom is a substitute for the old custom of immuring a living person in the walls, or crushing him under the foundation stone of a new building, in order to give strength and durability to the structure.[18]

In 1636, Jonathan Fayerbanke built a house in Dedham, Massachusetts. Helped by two hired carpenters, both probably fifty years old and from the north of England, Jonathan made his family's homestead with English oak and pink brick, with the old-fashioned and familiar Elizabethan architectural features from around 1600. Since Dedham was then a frontier, he included a hiding place and an escape tunnel from the house in case of attack, and a closet by the chimney to keep his gun powder dry. A gambrel-roofed addition was completed in 1648, and another, west wing around 1654. During reconstruction centuries later, a pair of slippers was found in the walls. This American custom to bring good luck had its antecedents: the old foundation rites.[19]

The London Bridge game is played lightheartedly. Two players face each other and join upraised hands to form an arch, imitating the bridge. The verses are sung by all the other players as they run under the arch, each holding onto each other and afraid that the arch will fall and capture him. The "prisoner" ensnared by the first two players is rocked gently back and forth in time as the verse is sung:

> Off to prison you must go
> You must go, you must go
> Off to prison you must go
> My fair lady.

The prisoner enters the game with "Oh, what has my poor prisoner done?"/ "Robbed a house and killed a man."/ "What will you have to set her free?"/ "Fourteen pounds and a wedding gown."/ "Stamp your foot and let her go." In the Hampshire version, the chorus sang "Off to prison you must go." In Cork, it was "Let everyone pass by but the very last one, and catch him if you can."

In pagan Europe, the drifter or local undesirable was put to death. Christianity brought a very gradual amelioration of the custom. Animals began to be slaughtered instead, or the person siezed would be allowed to pay a forfeit to escape certain death. The forfeit is also reflected in the modern game:

> Two players go away from the group secretly to choose bribes for their respective sides; such as a string of pearls for one side and a diamond necklace for the other side, or a span of black horses and an Arabian charger with gold trappings. The bribes having been chosen, these two leaders return to the group and raise their clasped hands to form an arch with their arms; then the group begins to sing the game and march through the arch. When the words "My fair lady-o" are sung, the two leaders drop their arms quickly around the player

just passing through the arch and, while everyone sings the chorus, the prisoner is led away far enough for the offers to be made by the leaders and a choice to be made by the prisoner without being heard by the others. When he had made his selection, he takes his place behind the leader whose gift he has chosen. They return to the group and the game continues till all the players have made their choice. A tug of war ends the game.[20]

The final tug of war may be the dramatic presentation of the clash between the deities for possession of the soul crossing the bridge at death. Pagan and Christian alike believed in the immortal soul of man.

> Ring around the rosie
> Pocketful of posie
> Blind man, blind man,
> We all fall down.

"Memento quod cinis es, et in cinerem reverteris." During the years of the bubonic plague, or the Black Death, in Europe, these words in the Latin must have seemed unnecessary: "Remember that thou art dust and wilt to dust return." The chances were good that the priest who spoke them was seen as unnecessary as well, for with four of every ten clergymen dead of the contagion in England from 1348 to 1350, many incompetents and mountebanks had joined the church. Sometimes even children were recruited for the priesthood. With one-third of Europe dead, the formal ritual was suspect and church attendance was down. Beneath an awful deity, lay piety and fanatic groups formed, like the Flagellants, who set out from village to village, covered with ashes, lamenting and lashing themselves. Their icons, groans, and burning incense made a dismal spectacle. Excess held illimitable sway.

The infective bacillus was one *Pasteurella pestis*, but without a sustaining germ theory, medieval people could only blame each other for the disaster. Before the advancing line of the plague, from Italy to France and Spain, then England,

Germany, and finally Russia, Jews were blamed for poisoning wells. They were burned at the stake—over papal protests—but all to no avail. Villages and cities were deserted by the fearful fleeing the horror, commerce was paralyzed, famine rife, and domesticated animals turned wild. The numbing and brutalizing effects of the plague, the neglect and despair, killed many who escaped the bacillus. In Genoa, six out of every seven people died.

In the gentle pastime "Ring around the Rosie," children hold hands and dance in a circle around a central figure, who stands still. The verse is sung, and with the final line, all fall down. There is perhaps no more poignant ceremony. The central figure represents the dread victim of the Black Death, standing silently. The circling, singing children seem almost to be trying to exorcise his malady. The victim is called the "rosie" because of the hemorrhages—the plague spots, dark on the skin—of the Black Death. The "pocketful of posie" or "pot of posie" was the flowers, garlands, and bundles of dried aromatic herbs used to mask the frightful odors of the dying. In some versions, the third line of the chant is "A-tishoo, A-tishoo"—imitating the sneezing of the victim, that being the last symptom of the disease to appear. According to an Italian legend, the custom of saying "God bless you" when someone sneezes began during the plague of Justinian, which raged for fifty-two years, A.D. 540–92. But the children's ceremony is apparently futile, for the victim spreads the contagion, and "we all fall down."

"Blind man, blind man" is also rooted in pathology. The invasion of the bacillus produced red, inflamed eyes and a marked intolerance for light—so much so that plagued people bandaged their eyes. The cast-out, wandering victims tended to be most active at night, to avoid the sun. In his movie *The Seventh Seal*, Ingmar Bergman shows us several people around a campfire at night. Someone approaches from the surrounding woods, and a brand is thrust forth to discover who it is. The victim throws up his hands to block the sudden light and retreats. He needs food, but he is driven away. It may be that the children's ceremony is a way of atoning for the necessity for such cruelty—a way to soothe the angry spirits driven from the fire. There were so many of them.

"Ashes, ashes" is yet another chant version. It was common to say, "Ashes to ashes, dust to dust/ If God won't have you, the Devil must." This seems to be a kind of lay response to the church's Latin rite on the first day of Lent, Ash Wednesday. The priest pronounces the words from Genesis "Remember, man, that dust thou art, and unto dust thou shalt return," while making the Sign of the Cross on the forehead of the penitent. The blessed ash is from the burned palms of the previous year's Palm Sunday. Ashes and sackcloth were ancient ways of showing grief, humiliation, and repentance for sin, as in the Book of Job: "And he sat down among the ashes."

With its stress on the necessity to prepare for a holy death, the Ash Wednesday ceremony may have had its origins in the plague of Justinian, which began at Pelusium in Egypt in A.D. 540, reached Byzantium in the spring of A.D. 542, and Rome in A.D. 590. In Rome, Pope Gregory the Great, a saint, "implored men to purge away their sins with weeping but not to give up hope, because God does not will the death, but rather the redemption, of sinners. . . . He recalled that God had spared Nineveh when its people did penance for three days, and proposed for Rome a similar period of prayer and repentance to be followed by a massive procession from each of the seven ecclesiastical districts of Rome to the Church of the Blessed Virgin Mary the Mother of Christ on the fourth day, the festival of St. Mark."[21]

The common people also associated ashes with the plague in ways that had nothing to do with religion: "It was also known that the eruption of Vesuvius which destroyed Pompeii had been followed by a plague, attributed by Dion Cassius to the volcanic dust and ashes. . . . There was a violent earthquake in January 1348, which shook Greece, Italy and neighboring countries."[22] The Black Death, most believed, was caused by atmospheric distemper. People thought that they could actually see the plague advancing when they watched a pale fog creep along a street. The answer everywhere was to purge the air with fire. The ancient Greek physician Hippocrates had prescribed this in the second *Book of the Epidemics,* and the papal physician Guy de Chauliac followed him. The members of the College of Physicians of Paris thought that the constellations "in union with the rays of the sun, acting through the power of fire," would "protect and heal the human race" with an "endeavor to break through the mist": "Accordingly, within the next ten days, and until the seventeenth of the ensuing month of July, this mist will be converted into a stinking deleterious rain, whereby the air will be much purified. Now, as soon as the rain shall announce itself, by thunder or hail, every one of you should protect himself from the air; and, as well before as after the rain, kindle a large fire of vine-wood, green laurel, or other green wood; wormwood and chamomile should also be burnt in great quantity in the market-places, in other densely inhabited localities, and in the houses. . . ."[23]

There was a kind of sympathetic logic in all these cures; the poisonous fire—or fever—in the body could be prevented by the purging fires burning the air. The burning of incense was universal. All these fires may well have helped, for the *Pasteurella pestis* has a low tolerance for heat when it is outside the body. This belief in fire persisted. Daniel Defoe says, in *A Journal of the Plague Year,* that people burned gunpowder, pitch, and sulphur in their houses and smoked tobacco. The abandoned houses of victims burned night and day. There were "ashes, ashes" everywhere. Sometimes—as it happened—there were people burned in the houses. This was part of a more particularly calculated purge, as at Mainz:

It is also reported that the execution fires there were so huge that the lead in the window-panes and the bells of St. Quirius' Church melted in the heat. The persecutions in Mainz appear to have been sparked off by the Flagellants who had entered the city in August and precipitated bloody quarrels with the Jews. It seems to have been frequently the case that the religious frenzy inspired by the Flagellants inflamed the suspicions and fears of the people into whose cities their processions came. At Mainz, and later at Speyer and Eslingen, to escape murder at the hands of fanatical crowds the Jews burned themselves to death in their own houses. At Eslingen, according to the Limburg Chronicle, the entire Jewish community gathered together in the synagogue, then set it on fire and perished together. Guillaume de Nangis says that mothers often threw their children on to the pile to prevent their being baptised, and then threw themselves into the flames. At Speyer, where the Jews had burned themselves in their houses, their bodies were collected, put into empty wine casks and rolled into the Rhine, lest they infect the air of the city; but the senate did not neglect to search the burned houses for treasure.[24]

Many people found the flagellants, with their sackcloth and ashes, barefooted, chanting, groaning, weeping, and tearing their hair, bleeding from scourging, burning incense and bearing icons, to be entertaining. But Pope Clement VI recognized their threat to church ritual and denounced them. The Brotherhood of Flagellants or the Brethren of the Cross was sincere and well ordered. Their ceremony attracted many—especially the new hymns, composed for the cross-bearers and sung in the language of the people. These "new songs were memorized and passed on to the extent that . . . in 1832 one of the hymns of the Flagellants was still extant in Germany in a variety of dialects."[25] The church persecuted the Flagellants because they believed that a direct appeal to God was possible without the intervention of the clergy—heresy.

Besides singing the forbidden new hymns, the common people turned to the ancient circle dances—pagan fertility rites—in the face of overwhelming death. Originally enacted in cemeteries by male plague victims, the Dance of Death gradually came to include women as well, with twenty-four people dancing in all.[26] The sight of children dancing around the dead may now strike one as a breach of propriety, but

> The medieval world regarded death as the liberation of the soul from the body and its entrance into Heaven. A popular dance, still the national dance of Aragon, was the *jota* in Spain; it was a feature of funerals, especially when the deceased was a child. The Flemish had their custom of dancing around the coffin of a young girl. The Slavonic funeral dirge, piped while a young man simulated death, with girls and women dancing round him, was thoroughly medieval. The Hungarian custom was to dance round a male mourner who was seated in the same room with the corpse.
>
> Cemetery dances were certainly connected with funeral dances. With regard to the celebration of the feast of St. Elined, Giraldus Cambrensis, in his *Journey through Wales*, wrote: "You may see there men or girls, now in the church, now in the cemetery, now in the dance which is led around the cemetery with song, suddenly falling to the ground, and at first as though in ecstasy and trance, then immediately as if in frenzy springing up, representing with their hands and feet to the people the work and whatever other things they had been accustomed to doing illicitly on feast days."[27]

These popular circle dances were not merely fertility rites of death and rebirth; they were carnivals of egalitarianism. The church despised them, but in the face of mass extinction, concessions were apparently in order. The Italian *carolare*, a ring dance with singing, was finally accepted by the church, grudgingly, in the fourteenth century. From *carolare* comes our "Christmas carol."

The dance beneath the gallows is the wildest dance of all. Beginning in Aix-la-Chapelle, in the streets of Aachen in midsummer 1374, and following quickly in Liege in Belgium and

Utrecht in the Netherlands, the Dancing Mania seized Europe:

> In the Rhineland . . . a new hysteria appeared in the form of a dancing mania. Whether it sprang from misery and homelessness caused by heavy spring floods of the Rhine that year, or whether it was the spontaneous symptom of a disturbed time, history does not know, but the participants were in no doubt. They were convinced that they were possessed by demons. Forming circles in streets and churches, they danced for hours with leaps and screams, calling on demons by name to cease tormenting them or crying that they saw visions of God or the Virgin or the heavens opening. When exhausted they fell to the ground rolling and groaning as if in the grip of agonies. As the mania spread to Holland and Flanders, the dancers appeared with garlands in their hair and moved in groups from place to place like the flagellants. They were chiefly the poor—peasants, artisans, servants, and beggars, with a large proportion of women, especially the unmarried. Sexual revels often followed the dancing, but the dominant preoccupation was exorcism of devils. In the agony of the times, people felt a demonic presence. . . .[28]

These dancers believed that the demons were successful because they had been invalidly baptised by priests living in concubinage. They sought to exorcise the evil spirits by going to chapels during the Feast of Saint John the Baptist. During the outbreak in Strasbourg in 1418, the victims were taken to the Chapel of Saint Vitus, an obscure third-century child martyr who was believed to be able to protect sufferers from convulsive disorders. "St. Vitus Dance" is now the popular term for the medical condition chorea, which expression is itself taken from the Greek *choreia* (dance). In Italy, the bite of the tarantula was believed to be the cause of the mania known as tarantism. The dancing served to work out the poison—we know the tarantella.

Four centuries later, Charles Dickens in *A Tale of Two Cities* described a furious and cruel ring dance of five hundred peasant revolutionaries by the prison wall during the Reign of Terror. He then commented, "No fight could have been half so terrible as this dance. It was so emphatically a fallen sport—a something, once innocent, delivered over to all deviltry—a healthy pastime changed into a means of angering the blood, bewildering the senses, and steeling the heart. Such grace as was visible in it, made it the uglier, showing how warped and perverted all things good by nature were become."[29]

There was a terrible struggle to comprehend the Black Death, never completely successful. Image and word struck deep, but always seemed inadequate: "The metaphor of plague as a blow of the sword or the sting of an arrow is deeply ingrained not only in Biblical literature but in the literature of Greece and Rome as well. Practically all the Hebrew words for plague (*Maggefah, Negef, Maga, Makkah*) indicate a blow. Our English word 'plague' and the German *plage* derive via the Latin *plaga* from a Greek word meaning a blow. The French *fléau*—a flail or a plague—embodies the same idea and is derived from the Latin *flagellum*. The Arabs speak of being "stung" or "pricked" with plague."[30] Priests pondered the words "O death, where is they sting? O grave, where is thy victory? The sting of death is sin; and the strength of sin is the law" from Paul's letter to the Corinthians. George Deaux observes that "folk literature of the period is full of parables of death and resurrection that may have derived some of their inspiration from the plague; one remembers, for instance, that Sleeping Beauty falls into a deathlike sleep after having been pricked with a needle and that, in a common figure of speech, the plague was spoken of as having pricked or stung its victims."[31]

Six hundred years ago, children danced to death, yielding the simple ritual, "Ring around the Rosie." So long as "we all fall down," there will be terror and the answering ritual. That student of medieval custom, Mark Twain, faced man's crippling capacity to feel guilt and terror and yielded to bitter pessimism. But after "Ring around the Rosie," the children rise up from the ground, joyous and laughing. The game enforces the knowledge that we too must rise up so early and know once again Saint Augustine's words *Volo ut sis:* "I want you to be."

Notes

1. Catherine Storr, "Why Folk Tales and Fairy Stories Live Forever," cited from *Suitable for Children? Controversies in Children's Literature*, edited and introduced by Nicholas Tucker (Berkeley and Los Angeles, California: The University of California Press, 1976), p. 72.
2. Michael Wood, *America in the Movies; or, "Santa Maria, It Had Slipped My Mind!"* (New York: Basic Books, Inc., Publishers, 1975). p. 18, cites Franz Kafka from *The Great Wall of China*.
3. Lord Raglan, "Myth and Ritual," cited from *Myth: A Symposium*, ed. Thomas A. Sebeok (Bloomington, Indiana: The Indiana University Press, 1958), p. 123.
4. Thomas S. Szasz, *The Manufacture of Madness; A Comparative Study of the Inquisition and the Mental Health Movement* (New York: Harper and Row, Publishers, 1970), p. 267.
5. Susan Sontag, "The Imagination of Disaster," cited from *Awake in the Dark; An Anthology of American Film Criticism, 1915 to the Present*, ed. David Denby (New York: Vintage Books, a division of Random House, 1977), p. 277.
6. William Butler Yeats, "The Circus Animals' Desertion," cited from *Selected Poems and Two Plays of William Butler Yeats*, edited and introduced by M. L. Rosenthal (New York: Collier Books, 1961), p. 185.
7. Eloise Hubbard Linscott (ed.), *Folk Songs of Old New England* (New York: The Shoe String Press, Inc., Archon Books, second edition, 1962), p. 2.
8. Ibid., p. 5.
9. Edward Darling and Ashley Montagu, *The Prevalence of Nonsense* (New York: Harper and Row, Publishers, 1967), pp. 158–59.
10. Iona and Peter Opie, (eds.), *The Oxford Dictionary of Nursery Rhymes* (Oxford: At the Clarendon Press, 1951), pp. 156–57.
11. Linscott, *Folk Songs of Old New England*, p. 5.
12. Opie/Opie, *The Oxford Dictionary of Nursery Rhymes*, p. 157.
13. Linscott, *Folk Songs of Old New England*, p. 34. In legends, the Devil is bribed with all manner of offers if he will spare bridges.

14. Opie/Opie, *The Oxford Dictionary of Nursery Rhymes*, pp. 270–71.

15. Ibid., p. 273: ". . . A record which appeared in the *Gentleman's Magazine* for September, 1823. A correspondent there wrote, 'The projected demolition of London Bridge recalls to my mind the introductory lines of an old Ballad, which more than 70 years ago I heard plaintively warbled by a lady who was born in the reign of Charles the Second, and who lived till nearly the end of that of George the Second. . . .' "

16. Linscott, *Folk Songs of Old New England*, p. 34.

17. Opie/Opie, *The Oxford Dictionary of Nursery Rhymes*, pp. 275–76.

18. James G. Frazer, *The Golden Bough: The Roots of Religion and Folklore* (New York: Avenel Books, Crown Publishers, Inc., 1981), p. 144. This work was originally published in two volumes in 1890 as *The Golden Bough: A Study in Comparative Religion*.

19. Carole J. Maconi, "The Fairbanks House," in collaboration with Arthur and Miriam Blood and Area Freeman Sidebotham (Southborough, Massachusetts: Yankee Colour Corporation, 1976), pp. 3–7.

20. Linscott, *Folk Songs of Old New England*, p. 35.

21. George Deaux, *The Black Death, 1347* (New York: Weybright and Talley, 1969), p. 35.

22. Ibid., p. 54.

23. Ibid., p. 52.

24. Ibid., p. 173.

25. Ibid., p. 182.

26. This Dance of Death was a popular theme in late medieval art, as in Hans Holbein's woodcuts. Usually in the form of a grotesque skeleton, Death leads all men and women to the grave. George Deaux (*The Black Death, 1347*, p. 208) adds that "typical examples show skeletons dancing about an open grave, leading children by the hand, kissing women before an open coffin, or leading a procession of the living in a formal dance, sometimes to the music of drums and violins."

27. John F. Burns and Jeremiah O'Sullivan, *Medieval Europe* (New York: F.S. Crofts and Co., 1946), p. 550.

28. Barbara W. Tuchman, *A Distant Mirror; The Calamitous Fourteenth Century* (New York: Ballantine Books, 1978), pp. 274–75.

29. Charles Dickens, *A Tale of Two Cities*, with an introduction by Edgar Johnson (New York: The Washington Square Press, Inc., 1960), p. 348.

30. Deaux, *The Black Death*, p. 15.

31. Ibid., pp. 210–11.

Additional Sources

Baldwin, James. *Nobody Knows My Name: More Notes of a Native Son*. New York: Dell Publishing Co., 1963.

Bone, Robert A. *The Negro Novel in America*. New Haven and London: The Yale University Press, 1958.

Brown, Dee. *Bury My Heart at Wounded Knee: An Indian History of the American West*. New York: Holt, Rinehart & Winston, 1971.

Coulette, Henri and Levine, Philip, eds. *Character and Crisis: A Contemporary Reader*. New York: McGraw-Hill, 1966.

Deloria, Vine, Jr. *Custer Died For Your Sins: An Indian Manifesto*. New York: Avon Books, 1969.

Drimmer, Melvin, ed. *Black History: A Reappraisal*. New York: Doubleday & Company, 1969.

Fredrickson, George M. *The Black Image in the White Mind: The Debate on Afro-American Character and Destiny 1817-1914*. New York: Harper & Row, 1971.

Gratus, Jack. *The Great White Lie: Slavery, Emancipation, and Changing Racial Attitudes*. New York: Monthly Review Press, 1973.

Henry, Jules. *Culture Against Man*. New York: Random House, 1963.

Hercules, Frank. *American Society and Black Revolution*. New York: Harcourt Brace Jovanovich, 1972.

Kracauer, Siegfried. *From Caligari to Hitler: A Psychological History of the German Film*. Princeton, New Jersey: The Princeton University Press, 1947.

Meier, August and Rudwick, Elliot M., eds. *From Plantation to Ghetto: An Interpretive History of American Negroes*. New York: Hill and Wang, 1966.

Nash, Gary B. and Weiss, Richard, eds. *The Great Fear: Race in the Mind of America*. New York: Holt, Rinehart & Winston, 1970.

Ogburn, Jr., Charlton. *The Mysterious William Shakespeare: The Myth and the Reality*. New York: Dodd, Mead & Company, 1984.

Osofsky, Gilbert, ed. *The Burden of Race: A Documentary History of Negro–White Relations in America*. New York: Harper & Row, 1967.

Ottley, Roi and Weatherby, William J., eds. *The Negro in New York: An Informal Social History*. New York: Oceana, New York Public Library, 1967.

Reik, Theodor. *Myth and Guilt: The Crime and Punishment of Mankind*. New York: G. Braziller, 1957.

———. *Pagan Rites in Judaism*. New York: Farrar, Straus & Company, 1964.

Spanuth, Jurgen. *Atlantis of the North*. New York: Van Nostrand Reinhold Company, 1980.

Talbott, David N. *The Saturn Myth: A Reinterpretation of Rites and Symbols*. Garden City, New York: Doubleday & Company, 1980.

White, Walter. *Rope & Faggot: A Biography of Judge Lynch*. New York: Alfred A. Knopf, 1929.

Velikovsky, Immanuel. *Earth in Upheaval*. Garden City, New York: Doubleday & Company, 1955. (By Alfred Einstein's associate at Princeton.)

Zinn, Howard. *A People's History of the United States*. New York: Harper & Row, 1980.